Antichrist in the Midst

Antichrist in the Midst

Lloyd K. Mosemann II

Antichrist in the Midst by Lloyd K. Mosemann II
Published by Creation House
A Strang Company
600 Rinehart Road
Lake Mary, Florida 32746
www.creationhouse.com

Unless otherwise noted, all Scripture quotations are the author's paraphrase.

Photo on back cover by Photography Unlimited, Inc., Allen Photography on July 11, 2005 at Myrtle Beach, South Carolina, www.allenphotography.net.

Cover design by Terry Clifton

Library of Congress Control Number: 2005939104
International Standard Book Number: 1-59185-995-6

First Edition

06 07 08 09 10 — 987654321
Printed in the United States of America

—Contents

—Introduction

THE AUTHOR OF these pages, Lloyd K. Mosemann II, claims neither academic nor theological credentials to authenticate the message of this book.

In the Heavenlies and *The Lie* were written during the late 1970s, and distributed to members of his congregation, while he was pastor of a local church. Several years subsequent to the completion of that ministry, in April, 1990, he wrote *Modern Parables.*

The documents gathered dust until 2005 when he discovered them, re-read them, and could scarcely believe that he had written them. At the same time he was impressed with the importance of making them available to all who would have "eyes to see, and ears to hear." Hence this book.

The message of this book will not be readily discerned by the intellect alone. The reader should ask the Holy Spirit to reveal the spiritual message for the church-at-large and for his/her life and ministry.

There is one important understanding required before you begin reading the meat of this book; viz., the relevance and significance of numbers in Scripture. Perhaps more than any other single academic consideration, the fact of numeric significance in Scripture confirms the authorship of the Bible as divine. No human could have organized such hidden mystery. At the same time, understanding the significance of numbers in Scripture enables the reader more fully to understand and appreciate what the Holy Spirit is saying. For that reason, a brief summary of the significance of numbers in Scripture is provided below. These are excerpts from *Number in Scripture* by E. W. Bullinger.[1]

1. *Unity, primacy, beginning.* Associated with God the Father in the sense of sufficiency or independence, which needs no other; e.g., first commandment.

2. *Difference*—generally in the sense of *testimony* or *witness*. However, can also signify *opposition* or *enmity*. Associated with *Christ the Son*; e.g., Rev. 1:5 calls Him "Faithful Witness."

3. Solid, real, substantive, *complete, entire*—reflected in the "*cube*"; e.g., holy of holies. In Scripture means *Divine Perfection*. Associated with the *Godhead* (three persons in one), and more particularly with the *Holy Spirit*. Note the replication of "holy, holy, holy" in Isaiah 6:3 and Revelation 4:8.

4. (**3** + **1**) That which follows the revelation of God in the Trinity; namely, His created works: *creation, earth*. Note that there are four regions to earth (north, south, east, and west), four seasons, material creation was finished on the **4th** day.

5. (**4** + **1**) Redemption follows creation! God's strength made perfect in the weakness of creation: *grace!*

6. (**4** + **2**) Man's world (**4**) with man's enmity to God (**2**) brought in.

   (**5** + **1**) Grace of God made of none effect by man's addition to it.

   (**7** – **1**) Man coming short of spiritual perfection.

   Note that man was created on the **6th** day. He is to labor

6 days and rest the 7th. Minutes in hour, hours in day, days in month, months in year are multiples of **6** and **4**.

7. *Spiritual perfection*; e.g., **7** spirits of Isaiah 11:2.

8. Literally means *to make fat* or *to superabound*. Especially has the significance of *new beginning*. Note that Jesus rose from the grave on the 1st day of the week, which was the **8th** day of Passover Week. Jesus was on a mountain 7 times before the cross, and the **8th** time after he rose. **8** is especially associated with resurrection.

9. Last of the digits. It marks the *end*, the *conclusion of the matter*. It denotes **finality** or **judgment**. There are **9** fruits of the Spirit, and also **9** gifts of the Spirit.

10. *Completeness of order*; *a whole cycle* has been completed. The 10 plagues on Egypt completed the circle or cycle of God's judgments. Also, denotes *human responsibility*: **10** commandments; tithe (meaning to give God $^{1}/_{10}$ th).

11. (**10 + 1**) or (**12 – 1**) *Disorder, disorganization, imperfection, disintegration*. Note **11th** hour in Matthew 20:6, 9, and concern at there being only **11** apostles (Acts 2:14).

12. *Perfection of government*; or, governmental perfection.

    (**3 x 4**) represents divine perfection as applied to God's creation. There are:

    12 patriarchs, **12** apostles, **12** foundations in heavenly Jerusalem.

13. *Rebellion*—see first usage in Genesis 14:4—in the **13th** year they rebelled.

14. (**2 x 7**) *Double measure of spiritual perfection*.

15. (**3 x 5**) Acts wrought by the *energy of divine grace*.

(**8** + 7) Indicates sometimes a reference to resurrection as a special mark of the *energy of divine grace.* Note that Bethany, where Lazarus was raised, was **15** furlongs from Jerusalem (John 9:18).

17. (**7** + **10**) *Perfection of Spiritual Order.* It is **7**[th] in the list of prime numbers (1, 3, 5, 7, 11, 13, 17). See Romans 8:35–39 and Hebrews 12:18–25 for **7** + **10**.

20. Generally interpreted as (**21** – **1**), indicating *expectancy.* See Genesis 31:36ff, 1 Samuel 7:2.

22. (**11 x 2**) *Disorganization and disintegration intensified.* Jereboam and Ahab each reigned **22** years.

24. (**12 x 2**) *heavenly government and worship.* See Revelation 4.

30. (**10 x 3**) Perfection of divine order as marking the *right moment.*

    Jesus was **30** when He commenced to minister (Luke 3:23); likewise, Joseph (Gen. 41:46) and David (2 Sam. 5:4) were **30** when they began.

40. Period of *probation, trial,* or *chastisement.* (**5 x 8**) points to the action of grace (**5**) ending in revival and renewal (**8**). Where it indicates *enlarged dominion* or *extended rule,* it is in harmony with (**4 x 10**). See Matthew 4:2 and Acts 1:2. See also Exodus 24:18.

42. Associated with *Antichrist.* See Revelation 11:2 and 13:5; See also, 2 Kings 2:23–24.

50. *Jubilee, or deliverance.*

70. (**7 x 10**) *Perfect spiritual order* carried out with all spiritual power and significance.

Both spirit and order are emphasized.

120. (**3 x 40**) *Divinely appointed period of probation.*

200. (**10 x 20**) *Expectancy, insufficiency.* See John 6:7, Joshua 7:21 with Psalm 49:7–9, and 2 Samuel 14:26 with 2 Samuel 18:9.

666. *Perfection of imperfection* (culmination of human pride in independence from God (**6**) and opposition to all He stands for and is (**3**). Remember that **6** is (**5 + 1**), the grace of God superseded by the corruption of man.

For an understanding of numbers in the structure of scripture, see *Theomatics* by Lucas and Washburn.[2] The following are notable examples:

"faith"	7 x 144; also, 800
"Kingdom of God"	8 x 144
"Kingdom of heaven"	20 x 144
"love of God"	777
"wrath of God"	666
"Jesus"	888
"law"	700
"I am the Way"	8 x 153

In Hebrew and Greek the letters had numeric value. They were used in lieu of separate numerals. For example, Greek *a* has the value of "1," Greek *p* has the value of "100," and Greek *r* has the value of "300." If there were a Greek word *apr,* it would have the value of the combined letters; that is, 1 + 100 + 300 = 401. As Lucas and Washburn declare in their book, "Theomatics scientifically proves that God wrote the Bible.... God has written His entire Word mathematically! Within the Bible there is a mathematical design, which reveals God's entire origin and authorship in such a way that the faith of Christians can be built up and strengthened."[3]

That was the Introduction. Now I am going to depart from tradition, and give you the Epilogue. I anticipate that after you have finished reading the book, you will ask one or both of the following questions. I am going to give you the answers in advance. It may be helpful if you keep the questions and answers in the back of your mind as you read.

Question #1

I thought that the Antichrist will be a world dictator who will persecute Christians. How can it be that the Antichrist is "in the midst" of the visible church on earth?

Answer

Romans 1:22–23: "Professing themselves to be wise, they became fools, and changed the glory of the incorruptible God into an image made like corruptible man..." In short, man has always been inclined to view God as if God were a man, with man's thoughts and behavior. Hence, the Greeks and Romans envisioned a family of gods, male and female, who lusted, were jealous, and fought, just like humans!

More relevant to the question at hand was the teaching/preaching of the Jewish scholars, rabbis, and priests who interpreted the Old Testament scriptures that predicted the coming of Messiah. They taught the people that the Messiah would come as an earthly king who would raise an army to fight and defeat the Roman enemy. They correctly interpreted that the Scriptures foretold the coming of Messiah, but they imagined Messiah from a human perspective, and not from the perspective of a God whose nature is love. When Messiah came as a lowly child, became a carpenter and itinerant preacher, and was crucified on a Roman cross, they missed the Messiah for whom they had been looking. Similarly, teachers of the New Testament have correctly identified the fact of Antichrist, but like the Jewish teachers they imagine him in the context of humanity rather than divinity. They are missing the reality of Antichrist "in the midst."

Question #2

You seem to indicate that there will shortly be another "move of God." What do you expect God to do next?

Answer

Obviously, no one knows the answer to that question. So far as I am aware, the previous moves of God were not publicly anticipated. On the other hand, it is clear that since 1517 God has been restoring the heavenly pattern in the church on earth. Hebrews 8:1–5 advises that Jesus Christ, who is seated on the right hand of the throne of the Majesty in the heavens, is minister of the "true tabernacle." The "true tabernacle" was initialized on earth when Moses was given instruction on how to fabricate the tabernacle in the Wilderness: "Moses was admonished of God when he was about to make the tabernacle; for, See, saith He, that you make all things according to the pattern shown to thee in the mount" (Heb. 8:5).

The heavenly pattern (the "true tabernacle") began to be restored to the church on earth when the Holy Spirit reestablished the "brazen altar"—the place of sacrifice for sins—when Martin Luther was given the revelation that salvation/justification is by faith, and faith alone, not by works!

Thereafter, other men of God were raised up who provided additional elements of truth. Restored to the church was the "laver" (wash basin)—the place of purification, sanctification, and cleansing—frequently considered a symbol of God's Word.

And, of course, the water baptism of adults by immersion was restored. John Calvin, Menno Simon, and John Wesley are the better known transmitters of elements of this revelation. In fact, the term "Methodist" came to be applied to the followers of John Wesley because they were committed to "methodical Bible study." Wesley ministered in the mid-1700s. Subsequently (in the 1800s), the holiness elements associated with the laver were revealed to, and enunciated by, men from whom came denominations and organizations such as the Wesleyan Methodists, Church of the Nazarene, Church of God (Anderson, Indiana), the Salvation Army and a few others.

In other words, it took from 1517 to the late 1800s to traverse the spiritual dimensions of the outer court of the tabernacle. Then in 1906 the lampstand (inside the holy place) was restored in the Pentecostal revival known as "Azusa Street." Now there was not just water baptism, and entire sanctification, but also the baptism in the Holy Spirit. Then things seemed to move more rapidly. The Latter Rain outpouring from Saskatchewan, Canada, in the late 1940s, and the Charismatic Revival of the 1970s restored the table of shewbread—the restoration of body ministry, the laying on of hands, healing, and the full operation of the gifts of the Spirit as in the days of the early disciples. For a time there was genuine recognition that loving one another in the Lord was more important than the historical traditions that had been codified in denominations. And that's where we are today.

What is left to be restored? The golden altar where a priest went alone; where he placed the sweet incense of worship on coals taken from the brazen altar; and where he made intercession for believers. The most famous golden altar experience was that of Zacharias (Luke 1:5–17) whose long ago prayer for a manchild was answered: "And you shall have joy and gladness; and many shall rejoice at his birth." The golden altar experience of Jesus is recorded in John 17 where he prayed for Christians alive today that "they may be one, even as we are one;

I in them, and you in me, that they may be made perfect in one; and that the world may know that you have sent me, and has loved them, as you have loved me..." (John 17:22–23). If this is the next move of God, it may not be broadly visible—individual Christians will be struck with the mandate to fast and pray that the ultimate manchild (Christ the Head, with the believers, His body) will be manifested. That will be the Second Coming.

May God bless you as you read. May we not be as the Jews who missed the Messiah, but as Paul who was struck blind to the world that he might see the reality of the living Messiah in the heavenlies.

1 — Modern Spiritual Parables

While listening to a very good Bible teacher (in 1990), his message awakened in me the need/desire to share some things. Following the teaching, there was a question and answer session. Predictably, two questions that were posed stood out: What do you think about AIDS? What do you think about abortion? Regarding the first, the speaker/teacher deplored homosexuality and indicated that AIDS is a punishment for the sin of homosexuality which is now rampant in our midst. Regarding the second, he indicated that abortion constitutes a bloodbath in our midst and that Christians must oppose it even to the point of martyrdom.

In my spirit I knew he had missed the point, as have most Christians. Ironically, in his message he had spoken about the mystery of parables and how they represent a means for God to present the truth to those for whom it is given to know the mystery of the Kingdom of God, and yet to keep the truth hidden from those who are "outside." Those outside will not hear or understand.

The open display of homosexuality and the increasing frequency of abortion which dominate our world, our nation, and our newspaper headlines are not new. They are certainly not unique to the present age or generation. Ever since Sodom and Gomorrah, homosexuality has been practiced and decried as sin. It was widely practiced and condoned during the age of the Roman Empire. It was clearly visible to the early church. In fact, Romans, chapter 1, in setting forth the litany of sin, places homosexuality second only to idolatry. I suspect, but cannot prove, that homosexuals have always constituted about 10 percent of the population. The practice may not have been as flagrant as now, but it has been with us. And, in fact, we know about it now only because of AIDS, a mysterious disease of very recent origin.

Similarly, abortion as baby killing is not new. I have personally been aware of this practice since I was a child. Moreover, it is wrong to say that abortion is an "American sin." Those who single out the United States as an object of God's wrath for this current wave of baby killing miss the mark, for abortion is probably more prevalent overseas than here; for in Europe and elsewhere abortion is an accepted, and perhaps even primary means of birth control.

A great wave of baby killing heralded the advent of the birth of Israel as God's chosen nation at the birth of Moses. A second wave of baby killing announced the birth of Jesus and the advent of the Christian era. These two great waves of baby killing were separated by two thousand years. It has now been two thousand years since the time of Herod and that second wave. Why should we be surprised to find it again two thousand years later? What we should ask is: "What does it mean or foretell?"

Hence, I believe we must look deeper than the obvious, superficial characterizations of homosexuality/AIDS and abortion that are so prevalent in Christian circles. Think about what happened. Forty years ago most people didn't even know that homosexuality and abortion existed. Today, they are mentioned in every newspaper, almost every day. Is this really just because we have become more sinful, or more tolerant of sin? Or, is this a divine metaphorical message to Christians and the church?

Following are some thoughts on these subjects. I trust that you will be blessed and encouraged by them.

Abortion

Abortion is "the expulsion of a human fetus before it is viable [within the first twenty-eight weeks of pregnancy]"; or, "the arrested development of an embryo or an organ at its [more or less] early stage"; or, "anything that fails in its progress before it is matured or perfected, as a design or project."[1]

Is abortion murder? Whether abortion is murder hinges on the further question, When does life begin? When does man become a living soul? In the case of Adam it is clear—"And the Lord God formed man of the dust of the ground, and breathed into his nostrils the *breath of life*; and man became a living soul" (Gen. 2:7).

It was the *breath of God* that gave Adam life!

The verb most commonly used in Scripture to describe the beginning of life is "conceive," as when David said, "In sin did my mother conceive me" (Ps. 51:5). Or, when the angel announced to Mary, "Behold, you shall conceive in your womb, and bring forth a son, and shall call his name Jesus." (Luke 1:31). Mary replied, "How shall this be?" And the angel answered, "The Holy Spirit [Holy Breath] shall come upon you, and the power of the Highest shall overshadow you" (Luke 1:34–35).

When the angel appeared to Joseph, he was even more explicit in indicating that conception is the beginning of life: "that which is conceived in her is of the Holy Spirit [Holy Breath]" in fulfillment of the prophecy that "the virgin shall be with child, and shall bring forth a son" (Matt. 1:20, 23).

To "conceive" is to bring into being a living soul which has within it the life of God and which has cognitive perception. When Mary, with the newly conceived life within her, visited Elizabeth "the baby [a fetus of six months] leaped in her womb." And Elizabeth spoke out with a loud voice, "Blessed are you among women, and blessed is the fruit [fetus less than one month old] of your womb... For, lo, as soon as the voice of your greeting sounded in my ears, the baby [a fetus of six months] leaped in my womb for joy" (Luke 1:41–44).

There is genuine life from conception! But, is the fetus of any value? Is a newborn baby of any value? Is the child of any value? Is the youth of any value? Not really, for at these stages of development the fetus/baby/child/youth requires attention and care. He/she may be a joy to the parents, but basically the fetus/baby/child is a burden to be borne and cared for. Even Jesus, who "increased in wisdom and stature, and in favor with God and man" (Luke 2:52) was essentially useless and nonproductive in the economy of God's Kingdom. Jesus literally disappears from view, and from the pages of history, from His conception and birth until His anointing as the Son of God at about age thirty. Two confirmations of Sonship are recorded:

1. To Jesus Himself—"You are my beloved son" (Mark 1:11; Luke 3:22). Mark displays Jesus as suffering servant; Luke displays Jesus as human/son of man. These required declaration/confirmation to Jesus!

2. To Israel—"This is my beloved son" (Matt. 3:17; John 1:34). Matthew displays Jesus as King; John displays Jesus as Son of God. These required declaration/confirmation to Israel!

Although some may disagree with me, I believe that Jesus, in his total humanity, was not confident. He certainly did not function in any special manner until God declared that He had attained full development, that He had matured, that He was perfect, that He had achieved Sonship! The death of Jesus at any time prior to this declaration and achievement, and His consequent entrance into his assigned ministry, would have represented an *abortion*.

It is clear, then, that abortion in the sight of God is not the death of innocent fetuses/babies/children, but rather it is the failure to achieve Sonship.

What is a "son"? In classical usage, a son is one who has matured to the point where he can take the place of the Father. Hence the Jewish tradition of bar mitzvah, which literally means "son of the commandment."

What is a "son" in the sight of God? The Scriptures are quite clear on this point—"For as many as are *led by the Spirit of God,* they are the *sons of God!*" (Rom. 8:14, emphasis added). Sons are those who have come out from the world and are separate (2 Cor. 6:17–18). Sons are "peacemakers" (Matt. 5:9). One cannot be a peacemaker amidst the jealousy and strife of the world, except one has come out from among the jealousy and strife of the world *and* is led by the Spirit of God.

Note well that, when we are "born again," we have only become part of the family of God—we are not yet sons! John 1:12 is very explicit, in that those who receive him (Christ), to them gives He authority to become the *children of God*: "who were born, not of blood, nor of the will of the flesh, nor of the will of man, but of God."

It is necessary and wonderful to be conceived as a new person in Christ by the Holy Spirit (Holy Breath), and thereby to be born a child of God, but this does not, per se, make us "sons of God." Sonship is for those who have achieved maturity—those who are "led by the Holy Spirit."

There are two well-known instances of the slaughter of babies and children recorded in the Scriptures. The first instance is very instructive. The purpose of this slaughter was not to kill Moses. The King of Egypt didn't even know that Moses existed—and, if he had known, doubtless he would not have feared a solitary man who could not even speak well. Rather, the King of Egypt feared the collective might of mature Israelites who represented, in his mind, a threat to the Kingdom of Egypt—which is a type, or symbol, of the established power structure in the world system.

The King of Egypt said, "Behold, the people of the sons of Israel are more and mightier than we" (Exod. 1:9). Pharaoh was afraid that the Israelites would continue to multiply and, then, when war occurred, would join with Egypt's enemies and fight against Egypt. Therefore, he set taskmasters over the sons of Israel, making them slaves, and afflicted them with great burdens. But the more the Egyptians afflicted them, the more the sons of Israel multiplied and grew. Hence, the King of Egypt was driven to a more drastic solution. He commanded that young boys should be killed, so that they would not grow into manhood (Sonship) and perpetuate and strengthen the might of the Sons of Israel (Exod. 1:10–16; Acts 7:19).

We know that Moses, by becoming an Egyptian, survived. It was not until he was fully forty years old when "it came into his heart to visit his brethren, the sons of Israel" (Acts 7:23), that he acknowledged his lineage. This was his "born again" experience. However, another forty years passed before Moses was anointed as a son in the presence of the Holy Spirit (burning bush) and given his ministry (Acts 7:30–36).

The story of Herod and Jesus is similar. Herod well knew the prophecies that a King of the Jews would be born. He and the power structure that he represented were directly threatened by the birth of the baby Jesus. Accordingly, he ordered that the children under the age of two should be murdered. This was a fulfillment of Jeremiah's prophecy, "In Ramah ("lofty places, heavenlies") was there a voice heard, lamentation, and weeping, and great mourning, Rachel weeping for her children, and would not be comforted, because they are not!" (Matt. 2:16–18).

These two massacres of children and babies occurred, respectively, two thousand years after Adam, and two thousand years after Moses. It is now two thousand years after Jesus. If each day, in God's sight, is as a thousand years (2 Peter 3:8), we are seeing the completion of the six day "work week." The sixth day, the day of man, the most recent one thousand years, has seen, beginning with the Renaissance, the perfection of humanity. In his own sight, man is perfect! World peace is about to be realized. Already, in 1990, there was talk that swords will be literally turned into plowshears (or space stations), so that man's works might further increase. Man has never had a greater glory, and his vision is of even greater achievement and glory—to conquer war, disease, space and even time. (Remember "666," the "perfection of humanity.")

Is it just coincidental that, at the end of another two thousand-year period, as man's system has again realized the relative perfection of Egypt and Rome, there is another massacre of infants—in this case, those not even born? And, if not coincidental, must there be some deeper message? This slaughter will end. God will see to that. Christians need not march and go to jail, for that is simply to employ the tools of the world system against the world system.

What must Christians do? What is the message of abortion for the church of Jesus Christ? Is there not a greater warfare? A warfare in the heavenlies? And, if so, what is the nature of the conflict, and do we have a role?

Clearly, we are living in End Times. All we need do is review again the progression of church history recorded in the letters to the seven churches in Revelation. The last of the seven church epochs described by John in Revelation 2–3 is Laodicea. The previous six epochs track historically with the progression of the church through history. Laodicea corresponds to the present age. What is Laodicea? Laodicea is comprised of two Greek words: *lao,* meaning "people" (hence, the English word *laity*); and *dicea,* meaning "sayings" (hence, the English words *diction* and *dictate*). Therefore, Laodicea is the Church Age characterized by "people's sayings" or "people's opinions."

There is no authority; there is no certitude; there is fear; there is hurt; there is doubt; there is weakness. Collectively, and individually, we are "neither hot nor cold," but "lukewarm."

We think we are blessed spiritually and have need of nothing. We have enjoyed a charismatic revival, new insight, End-Time revelation, and the accumulated orthodox wisdom of two thousand years of church history. What more could we learn? We are a superior people! Yes? No!

We are "wretched, miserable, poor, blind, and naked" (Rev. 3:17). We are given counsel in Revelation 3:18–22 to:

> Buy gold tried in the fire.
>
> Buy white raiment, that you may be clothed and that the shame of your nakedness is not apparent.
>
> Anoint your eyes with salve that you may see.
>
> Receive my love, my rebuke, my chastening.
>
> Be zealous and repent.
>
> Hear my voice.
>
> Open the door.
>
> Be an overcomer. (Note: This is the eighth instruction, symbolizing "new beginning.")

This is nothing less than a call to Sonship—in fact, it is a call to "come out." It is instructive that the King of Egypt was concerned that the Sons of Israel would not only "fight against us," but, in particular, would "get themselves up out of the land." Pharaoh did not want to lose these Israelites—they made good servants and slaves—and, he wanted to keep them "in."

There are three usages of the phrase "sons of God" that pertain to Christians in the Book of Romans.

1. *Beginning*—Those led by the Spirit of God are Sons of God (Rom. 8:14).

2. *Process*—Creation waits for the manifestation of the Sons of God (Rom. 8:19).

3. *Perfection/Completion*—"I will call them my people, who are not my people; and her beloved, who was not beloved. And it shall come to pass that, in the place where it was said unto them, 'You are not my people', there shall they be called the Sons of the Living God" (Rom. 9:25–26).

In Matthew 5:43–48 (compare to Luke 6:35) we are instructed:

> Love your enemies.
>
> Bless them that curse you.
>
> Do good to them that hate you.
>
> Pray for them who despitefully use you and persecute you that you may be the Sons of your Father who is in *heaven.*
>
> *Be perfect even as your Father in heaven is perfect.* (Perfect = fully developed, sanctified, full growth into Godly maturity = being led by the Spirit of God)

The tragedy of the Christian church in this Laodicean age, and the tragedy of Christians generally, is that so few, if any, of us are overcomers. Are we, like Paul, truly pressing on, seeking the prize that is a high calling in Christ Jesus?

There is one significant difference between the baby murders of Moses' and Jesus' day and the fetus murders of today. In those earlier instances, the murderers are opposers—they are external and separate from those who birthed the babies. In the murder of fetuses, the murderer is the parent—if not in deed, at least in will!

The question must be: "What is the spiritual significance of these current events wherein babies are murdered by their parents?"

The first two massacres symbolize the condition of the world system that opposes the people of God. Both Egypt and Rome were blind to an act of God being accomplished external to the world system within the people of God. In the present case of the abortion massacre, however, the act of murder is perpetrated on one's own offspring. If this is a message to the church, we must ask, "Is the church killing its babies? Is the real opposition to Christian growth and maturity now from within rather than from without? Are newborn Christians being destroyed, and thereby deprived of becoming mature or perfect to take their places as Sons of God?"

We begin the walk of faith as children—we are "born" of the Spirit (John 3:1–8). To live in the Spirit we must, "as newborn babies, desire the pure milk of the Word, that you may grow by it" (1 Pet. 2:2). In Romans 8, wherein sons are defined as "those led by the Spirit," there is a distinction made that we are mainly "children [not sons] of God" (Rom. 8:16). As children, we are called upon to "suffer with him" that we may also be glorified (received into Sonship) with Him (Rom. 8:17).

As children we can enjoy "glorious liberty" (Rom. 8:21), for the nature of children is to be without care, to romp and to play, to enjoy life.

Deuteronomy contains an interesting characterization of those who, as children, shall enter into the promises of God. "Your little ones... Your children who in that day had no knowledge between good and evil, they shall go in there, and unto them will I give it (the Promised Land), and they shall possess it" (Deut. 1:39). God spoke this to parents who had rebelled against the commandment of the Lord, and who had gone presumptuously up into the hill (Deut. 1:43). These parents, who knew the difference between good and evil, were condemned to continue wandering in the wilderness, which is a type of wandering in the world.

Note well that children have no need to know the difference between good and evil. This was the situation in the garden while Adam was still a "son of God" (Luke 3:38), led by the Spirit of God (Gen. 3:8). Adam had no need for knowledge of good and evil, and was expressly forbidden this knowledge (Gen. 2:17). When, presumptuously, Adam sought this knowledge, he was condemned to leave the garden, and the presence of the Lord, to wander in the wilderness.

It is no surprise, then, that Jesus says that those who are *greatest* in the Kingdom of heaven are those who become as little children—those who know not the difference between good and evil. Note well Matthew 18:1–6:

> To receive an innocent child [without knowledge of good and evil] is to receive Jesus.
>
> To offend "one of these little ones who believe in me" brings punishment: "It were better for him that a millstone were hanged about his neck and that he were drowned in the depth of the sea" (i.e., buried deep in the world, rather than dwelling in the Kingdom of heaven).

Can this really mean what it says? Can it mean that we are not to know the difference between good and evil?

Isn't it the purpose of the church and pastors to teach us these differences so we can do good and avoid evil? In 1 John, which probably says as much about the Antichrist as any other portion of Scripture, we are explicitly informed that there are deceivers and seducers within the church and that "the anointing which you have received of Him abides in you, and you need not that any man teach you; but as the same anointing teaches you of all things, and is truth, and is no lie, and even as it has taught you, you shall abide in Him."

Interestingly, there is only one place in Scripture where we are instructed concerning gatherings of the church—and, teaching the difference between good and evil is not mentioned! "How is it then, brethren? When you come together, everyone of you has a psalm, has a doctrine, has a tongue, has a revelation, has an interpretation. Let all things be done unto edifying"; that is, "building up one another in the faith" (1 Cor. 14:26).

This does not put someone "in charge"—it does not limit revelation or impartation to one or a few, but indicates that the Holy Spirit will move through each one; hence, even the children of the Kingdom will have something to share—praise God!

How does this compare with a typical gathering of Christians? In our gatherings there is almost always an emphasis on a "form of godliness" (2 Tim. 3:5). We condemn sin, and encourage good works. Implicit in most teaching and preaching is constant distinction between good and evil, as leaders seek to build up not our faith, but our conscience. This is law, not innocence. "Are you so foolish? Having begun [been born] in the Spirit, are you now made perfect by the flesh?" Does the Spirit accomplish miracles among you by the works of law [or ways of the world], or by the hearing of faith? (Gal. 3:1–5)

How we want to exalt man, and to be exalted ourselves. Increasingly in church gatherings, we literally applaud (clap hands) those who have done a good deed, said a good word, or sung a sweet song (2 Tim. 3:2). Pictures of pastors often appear in prominent places.

In 2 Peter it is predicted that these last days in which we live will be characterized by a lack of knowledge of our Lord Jesus Christ (2 Pet. 1:8–9), and by a listening to man. We are told that the children of God shall be treated as "merchandise" (2 Pet. 2:3). Folks shall "speak evil of things they understand not" (2 Pet. 2:12). Basically, Christians shall follow the way of

Balaam (that is, the ways of the world wherein all is done for profit using man's methods) (2 Pet. 2:15).

Peter says that those who bring children into the Kingdom shall do so by promising "liberty," but shall really bring the children into "bondage" (2 Pet. 2:19). "If, after they have escaped the pollutions of the world through the knowledge of the Lord and Savior Jesus Christ, they are again entangled in it, and overcome, the latter end is worse with them than the beginning." In other words, life will become more confusing and miserable than if they had never become Christians! "It had been better for them not to have known the way of righteousness than, after they have known it [having been born of the Spirit and having become children of God], to turn from the Holy Commandment delivered unto them" (2 Pet. 2:20–21).

Those who offend the little ones will have a millstone hung around their necks. Who are these offenders? It is those who inhabit Babylon (Rev. 18:21).

Babylon (city of confusion or many voices) is the church of Laodicea (the church of people's opinions or voices). We know that, in Revelation, the "woman" which represents the church is not only beautiful and glorious and births the Christ (Rev. 12:1–2), but also is fallen and corrupt and has made merchandise of God's people (Rev. 17:6, 18). Compare to Isaiah 1:21: *"How is the faithful city become an harlot?"*

It is the church, this harlot Babylon (Rev. 17:4–6), who is murdering her own children. "And a mighty angel took up a stone like a great millstone, and cast it into the sea, saying, 'Thus with violence shall that great city, Babylon, be thrown down, and shall be found no more at all'" (Rev. 18:21).

As we consider the widespread abortion in the world today, this is the *first message* we should understand: the church is killing its own, suppressing and binding them so that her children do not achieve the maturity of Sonship.

As we look at this current killing of babies in historical context, we also see a *second message*: there shall be a "man" who survives the killing, and who shall achieve maturity (Sonship), and who shall usher in the next great era in God's plan for the ages.

> You shall weep and lament, but the world shall rejoice; and you shall be sorrowful, but your sorrow shall be turned into joy. A woman, when she is in travail, has sorrow, because her hour is come; but as soon as she is delivered of the child, she remembers no more the anguish, for joy that a man is born into the world.
>
> And you now, therefore, have sorrow; but I will see you again, and your heart shall rejoice, and your joy no man takes away from you.
>
> —John 16:20–22

The immediate focus and fulfillment of this promise by Jesus relates to the confusion, sorrow and dispersion associated with Jesus' death—the promise looks forward to the birth of the church at Pentecost. But there may be a deeper meaning also—for the essence of God's nature is unchanging!

These same words could have been written to the sons of Israel as they sorrowed under the bondage of Egyptian slavery, opposition from Pharaoh, and the utter hopelessness of the massacre of their children.

These same words could have been written to the Jews of Herod's day. They, too, sorrowed under the bondage of Rome, opposition from Caesar and Herod, and the utter hopelessness of the massacre of their children.

These same words could be written to the Christians of our day who labor under bondage to laws, calls for money, and the oppression of unforgiving and jealously demanding elders, pastors, and priests, and who watch in amazement and despair at the widespread approval of baby killing.

In fact, these words have been written for our day:

> And there appeared a great wonder [sign] in heaven—a woman clothed with the sun, and the moon under her feet, and upon her head a crown of twelve stars. And she, being with child, cried, travailing in birth, and pained [waiting] to be delivered.
>
> —Revelation 12:1–2

> And the dragon stood before the woman who was ready to be delivered, to devour her child as soon as it was born. And she brought forth a male child, who was to rule all nations with a rod of iron; and her child was caught up unto God, and to His throne. And the woman fled into the wilderness [out of the church and into the world], where she has a place prepared by God, that they should feed her there 1260 days.
>
> —Revelation 12:4–6

> And the dragon...persecuted the woman who brought forth the male child. And to the woman were given two wings of a great eagle, that she might fly into the wilderness into her place, where she is nourished.
>
> —Revelation 12:13–14

> And the earth helped the woman.
>
> —Revelation 12:16

> And the dragon was angry with the woman, and went to make war with the remnant of her seed, who keep the commandments of God, and have the testimony of Jesus Christ.
>
> —Revelation 12:17

Who is this male child that shall be born, and whose refuge is not in the church but in the wilderness of the world?

> These are they who were not defiled with women [the harlot(s)]; for they are virgins. These are they who follow the Lamb wherever He goes. These were redeemed from

> among men, the first fruits unto God and to the Lamb. And in their mouth was found no guile; for they are without fault before the throne of God.
>
> —Revelation 14:4–5

The great promise and product of the Church Age is the Christ! Please read Isaiah 66. Note that the Head is in heaven (that is, Jesus) and the feet are on earth (that is, the sons yet living) (v. 1). It is to this man that the Lord will look (v. 2), a man that is poor and of a contrite spirit, who trembles at His Word. This man is contrasted with those who shall be deluded (v. 4), who when God speaks do not hear. The man to whom the Lord shall look shall be hated, and "cast out" by his brethren: but, he shall appear to your joy, and they shall he ashamed! (v. 5) Then, again, he presents the picture of a woman giving birth to the man-child (vv. 7–9), and concludes with a summary of End Times in the few verses that extend to the end of the chapter.

Read again Ephesians 1, especially verses 22–23, together with Ephesians 4:4–6 (see also, Ephesians 4:15–32):

> There is one body, and one Spirit…One God and Father of all, who is above all, and through all, and in you all.

The new man is a corporate being, the first fruits of God to Himself as He executes His plan for the ages: Jesus is the Head; mature sons constitute the body. This new man shall be delivered from the wilderness at the end of the Church Age, the same corporate man of Revelation 7 who comes out of great trouble/tribulation.

Abortion, then, is a sign of the times. It is a call to mercy and grace (that is, all encompassing love) that will secretly, in the bowels of the world/wilderness nourish and nurture the children of God to manhood/Sonship. Abortion is a sign of the promise that the full-bodied Christ shall arise and assume His place before the throne of God. Hallelujah! Amen.

Homosexuality

Homosexuality refers to sexual desire for those of the same sex.

Does God love the homosexual—the gay? Can the gay love God? Is the situation of gays hopeless from the perspective of biblical Christianity?

Most Christians would presumptively answer that, ipso facto, any gay is a sinner. "Yes," they would say, "God loves him/her, but salvation is dependent upon a change in one's nature such that same sex attraction is not just renounced, but also replaced by opposite sex attraction."

This view is predicated upon two assumptions: 1) that the Bible denounces homosexuality as sin (Rom. 1); and 2) that homosexuality is explicitly, or implicitly, a matter of an individual's own choice or election. Hence, it is postulated, that by a contrary act of the will, an individual person may choose no longer to be homosexual.

This is an easy view for those who are not gay. For gays, however, this view is more than discriminatory. For gays who know that, whether biological or psychological, they did not choose to be gay, and who have the same concerns about the mysteries of life and death as the SAD ("straight and dignified"), this doctrine—if true—is absolutely devastating, for it condemns them to an eternity of hell and damnation.

It should not be a surprise, therefore, to learn that most gays shut out of their life any thought of knowing God. Such a God cannot be a God of Love, and, therefore, is not worth knowing. What other way is there to know about God than to look at the lives and attitudes of those who claim that He dwells within them? In those who call themselves Christians, where is the compassion? Where is the love? Where is the understanding and support?

These are not easy questions to answer! But, let us begin with God. God is the Creator. God is Love. God is Light. So says the Bible. Moreover:

> For of him, and through him, and to him, are *all* things: to whom be glory forever.
>
> —ROMANS 11:36, EMPHASIS ADDED

I believe that the Living Bible makes it plain: "For everything comes from God alone. Everything lives by His power, and everything is for His glory. To Him be glory evermore."

God has a purpose in and for all of His creation, and for all of His creatures. All of God's creation shall conclude in Him as part of His glory. Elsewhere it says, "Every knee shall bow and every tongue confess that Jesus Christ is Lord!" In the past I did not understand God's purpose for gays. Although I can read and understand Romans 1:32 ("those who commit such things [i.e., homosexual acts] are worthy of death") as well as the next person, in my heart has been the conviction that there is a glorious purpose being served by the gay. My heart tells me that God loves both the gay and the "Straight and Dignified" (SAD). God desires for both the gay and the SAD to love and to worship Him.

The first ray of light was allowed to shine upon my understanding as, one day, I read John 9.

> And as Jesus passed by, he saw a man who was blind from his birth. And his disciples asked him, saying, "Master, who did sin, this man or his parents, that he was born blind?" Jesus answered, "Neither has this man sinned nor his parents, but [he is blind] that the works of God should be made manifest in him."
>
> —JOHN 9:1–3

The disciples had a legitimate question: "Why is it that some are born blind?" A mere accident it cannot be, for our Creator is a God of purpose and compassion. How similar is the oft asked question, "Why was I born gay?"

Jesus' answer is straightforward and simple. The man was born blind in order that the workings of God should be manifested—displayed and illustrated—in the man's life. This answer, in fact, throws light on the reason for all suffering. God has his own wise reasons for permitting sickness and disease, for having made each of us somewhat different and special. And, if God has a wise, though not necessarily immediately apparent, purpose to be served by affliction, in some way he will be glorified thereby.

Moreover, the purpose of God and the associated glory may not become evident for long years. From John 9:23 scholars conclude that this man had been blind at least thirty years!

Why did Jesus choose this man and this occasion to make this pronouncement, and to provide sight to a man blind from birth? The key is the conjunction "and" at the beginning of the ninth chapter of John's gospel, for the "and" indicates that this incident is connected with the events of chapter 8.

In John 8, Jesus has a startling encounter with the organized religious authorities (the priests and preachers) of his day. Chapter 8 opens with the religionists wanting to stone a woman who had committed adultery—clearly a biblical sin. But Jesus just as clearly indicated that no sin is worse than any other when He said, "He who is without sin should cast the first stone." And none did, but quietly moved away, leaving Jesus alone with the adulteress.

Jesus then turned and spoke to the religious leaders, saying, "I am the Light of the world; he that follows me shall not walk in darkness [blindness], but shall have the light of life." This provoked a lively discussion with the religionists, during which Jesus made the famous statement that, "If you shall know the truth, the truth shall make you free."

Jesus further asserted that He Himself is that truth, and that, "If the Son shall make you free, you shall be free indeed." From the context (John 8:34) we know that this refers to freedom from the bondage of sin (the knowledge of good and evil), for those in Christ know no sin. Understanding of this fact, that those in Christ know no sin, is crucial/fundamental, and we shall discuss it further below.

The religionists could not accept the *simplicity* and reality of Jesus as the Fulfillment of the Law, which permits all those who receive Him into their lives to be free from the bondage and penalties of the Law. Accordingly, in the last verse of chapter 8, just prior to the description of the man who had been blind from birth, it is recorded that the priests and preachers took up stones to throw at Jesus. But it is recorded that Jesus "hid himself... Going through the midst of them." In other words, the religious leaders were all around Jesus, but could no longer see Him—for they were effectively blind.

Jesus announced himself as the Light of the world, but the very persons who had been preaching and teaching to the people concerning his coming missed the reality of the coming. On the other hand, a poor beggar, blind from birth, with no pretensions to anything, and certainly not to religious wisdom, had his blindness dissolved, and he saw Jesus! Moreover, he saw Jesus not just as a human healer, but as the Son of God! (John 8:35–38).

> And Jesus said, "For judgment I am come into this world, that they who see not, might see; and that they who see, might be made blind."
>
> —John 9:39

Hence:

Natural blindness	=	**Seeing Jesus**
Natural seeing	=	**Spiritual blindness**

Moreover, Jesus said, "If you were blind, you should have no sin. But now you say, 'we see.' Therefore, your sin remains."

Hence:

Natural blindness	=	Seeing Jesus	=	No sin
Natural seeing	=	**Spiritual blindness**	=	**Sin remains**

In other words, the glory of God that was displayed through the blind man was at least two-fold:

1. The condition of the world's religious system as self-centered and earthy was exemplified—the religionists could not see spiritual truth or spiritual reality, and they were set aside by God. In fact, truth is deliberately hidden from them by God for their hearts are hard and without compassion.

2. The condition of the unchurched, the ones despised by the religious system, is revealed as hopeless. No human remedy is available. Yet, in the hopelessness of their situation, Jesus as Light made a difference. Jesus made the blind to see, and they worshipped the Lord God.

The duality here is significant. Blindness describes the condition of the world, and especially its religious system (which, incidentally, had originally been ordained and established by the Lord himself). At the same time, it is made clear that the man's blindness is not a result of his sin, nor of his parents' sin, but is part of God's purpose in establishing Jesus as the Light of the world.

The blind man's affliction is, miraculously, the very means or instrument by which God singles him out and establishes him in a special relationship both to the world and to Jesus. In fact, this blind beggar, when he could see, was able to teach the religious leaders a profound truth: If any man be a worshipper of

God, and does His will, God hears that man (John 9:31)! But, they didn't hear him!

This two-fold purpose in the healing of this despised beggar, blind from birth, is exactly the purpose for which God in this present hour has brought to such prominence the afflictions of homosexuals. Natural homosexuality (gayness), like natural blindness, illustrates from God's perspective the bankruptcy and unfruitfulness of the world and its religious systems. Moreover, gays, when their eyes are opened to see the wonder of God's purpose and love, which shall be displayed as His Glory throughout eternity, will see that they have much in common with the God of the Ages, and will understand God's desire and purpose to take for Himself a groom (Jesus) and bride (the spotless church) as His eternal dwelling place.

Whether homosexual or heterosexual, there is more to life than sex!

The self-righteous Christian view is that heterosexuals confine sex mainly to marriage, exercise self-discipline, and spend most of life's hours in pursuits other than pure sex. The same self-righteous Christian view is that homosexuals are preoccupied with sex, are constantly seeking opportunities for sex, and view all situations from a sexual perspective.

Doesn't this sound ludicrous on its face? Gays will tell you that they seek to enjoy the fullness of life, in which sexual feeling and contact is no more or less important than for other healthy humans. There is a distinction, therefore, which should be made between the gay's nature or personality, and the gay's sex life. It is just as conceivable, or inconceivable, for the homosexual to be celibate, at least insofar as a physical relationship with another human being is concerned, as it is for a heterosexual.

In searching the Scriptures one notes almost immediately that virtually all references which relate to the gay lifestyle are to sexual practice rather than to personality or inherent nature. The one obvious reference to inherent nature is found in Matthew 19:3–12, specifically verse 12.

In Matthew 19 we find the disciples asking Jesus about divorce, and he teaches them about marriage:

> And he answered and said unto them, "Have you not read that He who made them at the beginning, made them male and female; and said, For this cause shall a man leave father and mother, and shall cling to his wife, and they two shall be one flesh? What, therefore, God has joined together, let no man put asunder."

In effect Jesus teaches that marriage is a sacred symbol without practical provision for divorce (compare to Ephesians 5:22–32).

The disciples, all males, thinking that marriage without divorce is like a prison without escape, exclaim that "It isn't good to marry!" In other words, failing to believe that two can truly become one wherein divorce is an irrelevant consideration, they opined that marriage should be avoided. In response to their concern, Jesus makes this statement:

> All cannot receive this saying [i.e., male and female shall become one flesh], except they to whom it is given. For there are some eunuchs[1], who were so born from their mother's womb; and there are some eunuchs, who were made eunuchs by men; and there are some eunuchs, who have made themselves eunuchs for the Kingdom of heaven's sake. He that is able to receive, let him receive.

---

[1] Eunuchs, literally, are men who have been castrated. However, the word "eunuch" by extension, also is used to describe a man who has no desire for women, or even a man who is celibate by choice.

With regard to a person's sexual orientation, Jesus clearly recognizes that some are born that way, and some are made that way by men. The current arguments whether homosexuality is innately biological, or whether it is largely learned behavior from the way the person was treated by parents and friends, are mostly irrelevant. In plain fact there have always been those who are innately gay! A third category exists—those who have put the desire for sex, whether toward male or female, under complete subjection because of their spiritual life. These latter treat their physical nature as a possession to be lightly regarded (compare to Philippians 2:6–7) in deference to total self-control for spiritual ends.

The only other mention of "eunuch" in the New Testament is recorded in Acts, chapter 8. Before we turn to Acts, however, we should note that "eunuchs" were highly regarded by the Lord in the Old Testament. In Isaiah 56:4–5, eunuchs who "keep My sabbaths" and "choose that which pleases Me," and who "take hold of My covenant" will receive a "place and name" in the House of the Lord better than if they had had sons and daughters: "I will give them an everlasting name, that shall not be cut off." In Jeremiah 38:7–13 it was a eunuch whose name means "servant of the king" that rescued Jeremiah from the dungeon. Moreover, from Daniel 1:3–18 a pretty good case can be made that Daniel was a eunuch! Clearly, the Lord did not write off the homosexual as have so many Christians in this age of Laodicea.

In the New Testament "eunuch" is used eight times. You will recall that numeric symbolism is an integral part of the inspiration of Scripture, both providing confirmation of the Scriptures having been written under divine inspiration, and also providing greater insight into the fuller meaning of the Scriptures. These are the eight usages:

Matthew 9:12 (1–3)

Acts 8:27 (4)

Acts 8:34 (5)

Acts 8:36 (6)

Acts 8:38 (7)

Acts 8:39 (8)

The first three usages, which we have already seen in Matthew 19:12, correspond perfectly to the meaning of the numbers "1," "2," and "3."

1. Origin or beginnings: "Born eunuch"

2. Process, manipulation: "Made eunuch by men"

3. Perfection, completion: "Eunuch for Kingdom of heaven's sake" (Note: "3" also refers to the work of the Holy Spirit. It is only by the power of the Holy Spirit that this latter can occur.)

Let us notice, then, the story of the eunuch in Acts 8.

4. The eunuch was black (Ethiopian). He was a man of great authority and responsibility, who had charge over all the treasure of the Queen of Ethiopia. Furthermore, he had come a great distance to the great cathedral in Jerusalem to worship the true God.

Clearly, here was one gay man who was highly respected and important. He was a double minority, even in that day, for he was both black and homosexual. But his heart was open toward God, and he sought to worship Him.

5. While returning from Jerusalem to Ethiopia, this gay man was reading the Bible. As he was reading, Philip, who had been one of Jesus' disciples, happened along and

asked if the gay man understood what he was reading. The Ethiopian took advantage of this opportunity to ask a question.

6. As Philip and the eunuch traveled along in his carriage, they came to a body of water. Apparently, Philip had been introducing the Ethiopian to the person of Jesus Christ, including the reality of His death and resurrection. In fact, he must have indicated that a person can identify with death to sin and with resurrection to newness of life in Christ through the medium of water baptism.

In any case, the gay man said, "See, here is water. What does hinder me to be baptized?" And Philip answered, "If you believe with all your heart, you may." And he responded, "I believe that Jesus Christ is the Son of God."

You see, whether homosexual or heterosexual, the issue is the same. The matter of substance is not personality, nor skin color, nor lifestyle, nor wisdom nor knowledge, nor power nor authority. The area of concern is not the thoughts of the mind, nor the desires of the flesh, but the inclination of the heart toward God!

The only issue for the heart, which is our innermost being, is the sufficiency of Jesus Christ as our intercessor before the throne of God. Hallelujah, what a Savior!

7. And so, "They both went down into the water, both Philip and the eunuch; and Philip baptized him."

The number seven in Scripture stands for "spiritual perfection." In this act of faith, the black gay man was perfected. He was still black; he was still gay. He was still very rich and important. He could also have been very poor and insignificant. He could have been a supercilious straight man, or an unconscionable womanizer. But, in this action of faith, his heart was transformed and perfected. As surely as Jesus, when He arose from the grave, displayed a new and spiritual body, so also did that gay man when he came forth from the watery grave. In fact, the term *baptize* derives from the Greek word *baptizo,* which was used to signify the dyeing of a garment or piece of cloth—it was still the same cloth, but had been transformed and given a new appearance!

> 8. "And when they were come up out of the water, the Spirit of the Lord caught away Philip, that the eunuch saw him no more; and [the eunuch] went on his way rejoicing."

The number eight in Scripture stands for "new beginning." Jesus, for example, rose from the grave on the eighth day of the week. Jesus was on a mountain seven times before the cross, and an eighth time after He arose. Resurrection in Christ is a new beginning; it is new life!

The black gay man, who had made the long and dusty journey to the church of his choice at Jerusalem, had come away empty-handed. But his heart was still seeking after God. And God met him where he was: in a chariot, returning slowly homeward through the dusty desert of the Gaza Strip. From the encounter with God the eunuch became a new creature in Christ, and he went on his way "rejoicing." He was still a eunuch, for nothing outward had changed; but, in his heart, he knew that he was a new creation.

In summary, the nature of the homosexual person does not bar his finding, knowing, and worshipping God. Why, then, with the example of the Ethiopian so clearly recorded in Scripture, do most Christians view gays with utter contempt and revulsion?

In part, this attitude is fed by the feeling of superiority and pride associated with any majority; and also by the need of most persons to justify themselves, at least in their own eyes, as better than someone else. (Hence, the counter response of an oppressed minority frequently is to proclaim its own pride, as *black pride,* or *gay pride.* But pride is clearly not a Godly virtue, and is hardly the response to someone else's pride, no matter how oppressive.)

On the other hand, there are also good and gentle Christian souls who seek to live a life of love and caring, and who feel that they dare not extend compassion to gays.

These attitudes, whether out of pride or fear, are rooted in two well-known passages of Scripture pertaining to the sin nature of man; i.e., the story of the destruction of Sodom, and the introductory chapter of Romans. In Romans 1:24–32 it is recorded that "they who commit such things," referring to sexual relations of woman with woman and man with man, "are worthy of death." It is essential, therefore, that we consider these passages in some depth.

The destruction of Sodom is recorded in Genesis 18:16 through 19:29. Of special interest are 18:20–21:

> And the Lord said, "Because the cry of Sodom and Gomorrah is great, and because their sin is very grievous; I will go down now, and see whether they have done altogether according to the cry of it, which is come unto me; and if not, I will know."

Sodom (which means "fettered") and Gomorrah (which means "bondage") had a great cry. From comparing the use of this particular Hebrew word *cry* in other Scriptures, we see that this was really a complaint. Moreover, their sin represented a "heavy load," for this is the literal meaning of the Hebrew word translated *grievous.*

As regards our understanding of God's purpose for bringing the gay lifestyle to prominence in our day, perhaps the most significant phrase in this passage is "whether they have done altogether."

Let there be no doubt that God has purposely and deliberately brought the attention of every thinking man, woman and child to the reality of gay life! Although homosexuals have always constituted a significant percentage of our population, it required the advent of AIDS to force society to recognize and acknowledge the existence of its gay subculture. Now, "gay" is on the pages of every newspaper almost every day. The enigma is why so few of our nation's leaders, whether political, economic or religious, have asked the question, "Why, God? What are you trying to tell us?"

Altogether in "whether they had done altogether" is an interesting word that can be translated "consummation." It literally means "to be quite done," "to be finished," "to be brought to a full end." The second usage of this Hebrew word is found in Exodus 11:1, wherein the final, tenth plague was to be perpetrated upon Pharaoh and Egypt so as to set the stage for the deliverance of Israel:

> He shall surely thrust you out from here altogether.

Probably the most famous usage of the term *altogether* or *consummation* is the eighteenth (found in Daniel 9:27). The number 18 has the connotation of "bondage." Bondage can be defined as a "state of being bound by or subject to external control." The number 18 can be composed by 9 x 2 or 6 x 3. You will recall that "9" denotes "finality or judgment," and "6" is the number of "man." Accordingly, 9 x 2 is "witness to finality," and 6 x 3 is "wholly man." Together they clearly signify that "man carries a heavy load." Note the correspondence of this significance with God's view of Sodom and Gomorrah as recorded in Genesis. Specifically, he saw that they were carrying a "heavy load" of sin.

Daniel prophecies that the end of the age will be tied to an overspreading of religious abominations leading to desolation "…until the consummation." The significance is heightened because Jesus, in His teaching on the end of the age (Matt.

24:15) asserts that "when you, therefore, shall see the abomination of desolation, spoken of by Daniel the Prophet, stand in the holy place..." From other scriptures, especially 2 Thessalonians 2, we know that this "holy place" is the visible, institutional church. There is much reason to believe that it refers specifically to the Laodicean church period, wherein we find that, chronologically, we are now within the "holy place" insofar as fulfillment of tabernacle symbology is concerned.

Accordingly, no one, gay or sad, homosexual or heterosexual, should take lightly the existence of the large gay community in the world in these days. Elsewhere in Daniel (12:4), it is made clear that the "time of the end" of the age shall be a time when "many shall run to and fro, and knowledge shall be increased." Men and women, gay and sad, by car or plane or space shuttle, today cover more miles in a day than Jesus, or even Marco Polo, or Abraham Lincoln, or Franklin Roosevelt, could travel in an entire lifetime.

And knowledge has increased! Historians used to count "knowledge" in terms of the number of books produced, or by the number of people who could read. In the twenty-first century knowledge is not just the number of books on library shelves, but more importantly the breadth or scope of knowledge, and the accessibility of that knowledge. Nuclear physics is an example of the former, and the ubiquitous computers and cell phones are examples of the latter. By any definition, we seem to be living in the "time of the end"!

What was the sin of Sodom? Was it sodomy? There is no doubt that sodomy was practiced in Sodom:

> And they [the men of Sodom] called unto Lot, and said unto them, "Where are the men who came to visit you this night? Bring them out unto us, that we may *know* them." ["To know" is a scriptural euphemism for intimacy associated with sexual intercourse.]

But frequently in the Scriptures what appears on the surface may not be the whole truth, the entire reality! What was the "cry," the complaint, of Sodom? What was the heavy load they carried? To understand this deeper truth, we must study Romans 1.

It is obvious, however, from the account in Genesis that the actions of the men of Sodom were to oppose Lot and the angels of the Lord. There was no place in their perspective for God. Hence, there is already in the Genesis account clear evidence that the root sin of Sodom was *human self-sufficiency!*

The sin of "self" (that is, to become a god unto oneself) is the true original sin associated with the Garden of Eden. This is evident from Genesis 3:5, where Satan tempts Eve with the promise that, in the day when her mind is opened to include the knowledge of good and evil, "you shall be as God…"

When man becomes a sufficiency unto himself, there may be a place for religion, but there is NO place for God Himself. There is barely a place for other men. Hence, the litigious spirit of complaints one against another. When each man must cope by himself, there is a sense of bearing a heavy load, or being "bound" and "fettered," as the meaning of the names Gomorrah and Sodom imply. One could argue that the "heavy load" they bore was the weight of sin and judgment. But to trust in oneself is the essence of sin.

So, the men of Sodom opposed the men of God and sought to seize and to exploit them. It is recorded, then, that the men of God (angels of the Lord):

> Smote the men who were at the door of the house with blindness, both small and great [that is, both youthful men and older men]; so that they wearied themselves [groping] to find the door.
>
> —Genesis 19:11

The parallel with the emphasis on blindness in the New Testament is striking. Not just the perspective in John, chapters

8 and 9 that we saw earlier, but it is noteworthy that, by far, the type of miracle most often performed by Jesus was the healing of blindness.

Blindness is the failure to see the wonder and purpose of God, and therefore to consider man an end unto himself. Hence, even when man gropes to find a deeper reality—for example, at the door of Revelation 3:20—he misses the way.

As in Jesus' day, and as prophesied by Daniel for our day, there is no greater blindness than of those who put their trust in religious institutions. Just like the Ethiopian eunuch who went seeking God in the churches of Jerusalem, they come away empty-handed.

In the person of Jesus Christ, God has offered himself as the "Way, the truth and the life"—there is no other way to the Father (John 14:6). God offers himself as man's sufficiency, willingly substituting His divine wisdom for human responsibility.

Let us turn, then, to Romans where we see a full and complete explanation of man's need, and of God's total and absolute sufficiency to meet that need. The key to the Book of Romans, and to an understanding of God's nature, plan and purpose is this: "The just shall live by faith" (Rom. 1:17; Hab. 2:4; Gal. 3:11; Heb. 10:38).

Actually, this translation is misleading, for it implies a work or effort by man—that of exercising some active initiative known as faith. The meaning, however, is more clearly seen in the Hebrew text of Habakkuk 2:4 (emphasis added):

> Behold, his soul that is lifted up [in self-sufficiency and pride] is not upright in him; but the just [that is, those at peace with God] shall live by His [God's] *faithfulness.*

We need not weary ourselves, groping as blind men to find a door, in order to be at peace with God! Being at peace with oneself and with God does not depend on human activity, but rather depends upon the faithfulness of God. He never fails! All that we, as humans, need to do is to rest in His sufficiency.

The beauty and wonder of just resting in the faithfulness of God was the special privilege of Adam in Eden. Recall that there were in the Garden of Eden two special trees: the Tree of Life and the Tree of the Knowledge of Good and Evil. (See Genesis 2:9.)

Man was not forbidden to eat of the Tree of Life, but was forbidden to eat of the Tree of the Knowledge of Good and Evil (Gen. 2:16–17). The Tree of Life was the source of immortality. By feeding on the Tree of Life man could live in peace, without guilt or fear, blissfully ignorant of what constitutes good and of what constitutes evil.

While feeding on the Tree of Life, and knowing not what is good and what is evil, man was not held accountable for sin—because he knew no sin! Whatever man desired was, in effect, legal and acceptable. Man was without the guilt of sin because he knew no sin. When man, however, chose to become as God, this situation changed.

Man, by feeding on the Tree of the Knowledge of Good and Evil, activated his conscience. Man became subject to external, moralistic codes of behavior necessary to govern his relationships with other men and with God. Why was this so? Because he was no longer feeding from the Tree of Life!

From the Tree of Life man had received the very essence of God's nature, which is innate, unconditional, unselfish love. Without love, man needed law. But law has no life to give! As a result, there was no power to obey the law, and soon the law was broken when Cain killed his brother over a difference in religious doctrine. And thus it has ever been. Man professes to love God and to love man, but fights to the death for his own parochial view of God's plan and purpose—and the abominations of desolation in the holy place accumulate until the consummation.

In Romans 1, the above recitation is essentially reiterated. Somehow man must begin again to feed on the Tree of Life and to scorn the knowledge of good and evil. This is nothing more, nor less, than living by the continuing faithfulness of God toward His creation.

The mechanism provided by God was the sacrifice of Jesus Christ who, as a perfect man created anew by God as the second Adam, fulfilled the Law and became, in effect, that Tree of Life ("Bread of life," John 6:32–35) for all who feed upon Him. In other words, we need not know the law, nor have knowledge of good and evil, because we can be "led of the Spirit" (Rom. 8:14).

See also John 15:5 where Jesus compares himself to a vine/tree and individual Christians to the limbs or branches: "I am the Vine, you are the branches; he that abides in Me, and I in him, the same brings forth much fruit; for without Me you can do nothing."

Paul's purpose in writing Romans, therefore, is to demonstrate that man alone is hopeless, blind, and bound, just as the men in Sodom were. Paul begins by recalling man's history from the earliest times when he truly "knew God" (Rom. 1:21). Again, the use of the verb "to know" implies an intimacy on the order of a sexual relationship between humans.

Why did man, when he knew God intimately, fall away from this intimacy and assume a nature that is all "ungodliness and unrighteousness"? (v. 18) This falling away was progressive:

- They did not honor and glorify Him as God/Creator (v. 21).
- They were not thankful to Him (v. 21).
- They became futile and godless in their thinking, abandoning the knowledge which had been imparted to them by divine revelation, and were guided instead by their own vain imaginings and foolish speculations concerning the nature of things (v. 21).
- Hence, their hearts were darkened as by blindness (v. 21).

- Their worldly wisdom which they prized so highly was nothing but foolishness in the sight of God (v. 22). (Compare to 1 Corinthians 1:18–3:23.)

- They attributed to God human personality and traits, and even those of animals, by portraying him in images/ idols and worshipping Him in the manner that would be desired by a human king (v. 23).

- Wherefore, "God also gave them up to uncleanness through the lusts of their own hearts, to dishonor their own bodies between themselves" (v. 24).

- They exchanged the truth of God for a lie, "and worshipped and served the creature more than the creator" (v. 25).

- For these reasons God "gave them up unto vile affections; for even their women did exchange the natural use for that which is against nature; and likewise also the men, leaving the natural use of the woman, burned in their lust toward one another, men with men working that which is *unseemly,* and receiving in themselves that recompense of their error which was fitting" (vv. 26–27).

From this progressive description of man/woman becoming *blind* to the person and nature and wisdom of God, we see that homosexual activity is an expression of a deeper attitude of the heart which ignores the reality of a loving, compassionate and interested Creator/God who desires intimacy with His creation.

Note that the progressive result of making God man-like in our thinking (compare present argument as to whether God is "he" or "she" or "he/she") is to work that "which is unseemly." The only other use of this Greek word "unseemly" in the New Testament is Revelation 16:15 where it refers to those who are spiritually "naked," and says that their "shame" (unseemly) shall be seen!

This use of the Greek word for *unseemly* or *shame* only twice emphasizes that there is special significance for us to notice. This provides confirmation of a careful reading of Romans 1:27–32. The careful reader will notice an important point ignored by most Bible readers. Specifically, homosexuality is not the only manifestation of this attitude of the heart and mind which does not grasp the knowledge of God. This knowledge of God comes only when we are "rooted and grounded in love" that we might know Christ and the fullness of God (Eph. 3:17–19).

Self-centeredness and human self-sufficiency engender not only homosexuality, but these human behaviors as well (Rom.1:29–32):

1. All unrighteousness
2. Fornication, iniquity
3. Wickedness
4. Covetousness, grasping greed
5. Maliciousness
6. Envy, jealousy
7. Murder
8. Strife
9. Deceit, treachery
10. Malignity
11. Whispering, gossiping
12. Backbiting, slandering
13. Hating God
14. Insolence
15. Pride, arrogance
16. Boastfulness
17. Invention of evil things
18. Disobedience to parents
19. Lack of understanding
20. Covenant breaking, lack of conscience, faithlessness

21. Lack of natural affection, heartlessness, love-lessness
22. Implacability, inflexibility, stubbornness
23. Lack of mercy

> And even as they did not like to retain God in their knowledge, God gave them over to a reprobate mind, to do those things which are not seemly [that is, to display the 23 characteristics listed above].
>
> —Romans 1:28

> Though they are fully aware of God's righteous decree that those who do such things deserve to die, they not only do them themselves but approve and applaud others who practice them.
>
> —Romans 1:32, AMP

The number "23" is the ninth primary number. It signifies absolute finality. We see, therefore, that the conclusion "*that those who do such things deserve to die*" is affirmed by the numerical structure of the Scriptures.

There are two obvious thoughts which should occur to us from the foregoing outline of the first chapter of Romans which ends with this list of twenty-three, and the judgment of death upon those who do these things.

1. Gay behavior is not the only one of man's historical behaviors with which God has been/is now displeased. Moreover, gay behavior is not the only displeasing behavior that is very much with us today. In fact, the other twenty-three, including pride and gossiping, are much more pervasive and prevalent in society, and among Christians, than gay behavior is ever likely to be!

Moreover, Paul writes another chapter and a half in Romans to emphasize this very fact, concluding in 3:10–11: "there is none righteous, no, not one: there is none that understands, there is none that seeks after God."

2. Gay behavior is singled out for first and separate mention as illustrative of man's propensity/inclination to "worship and serve the creature more than the creator" (Rom. 1:25). We must consider the significance of this special attention to gay behavior, but more on this presently.

Let us first consider these mournful passages: "worthy of death" (Rom. 1:32), "you are inexcusable, O man" (Rom. 2:1), "there is none righteous" (Rom. 3:10). The overall context of God's plan for man as revealed in the totality of Romans is that human behavior is depraved and unseemly, and that we shall stand naked and ashamed before our Lord except as we abide in His Grace. Let us, therefore, briefly look at the totality of Romans.

Outline of Romans

Overall theme

Man should live only by the faithfulness of God (1:17).

Man's deeds deserve death.

They who commit such things are worthy of death (1:32).

No man is righteous (no man deserves life).

There is NONE righteous, no, NOT ONE (3:10, emphasis added).

Man is justified (receives "life") by faith alone apart from deeds.

Man is justified by faith apart from deeds of the Law (3:28).

Knowledge of good and evil brings death.

By one man [Adam] sin entered the world, and death by sin, and so death passed upon all men, for ALL have sinned (5:12, emphasis added).

By faith death occurs in Christ, bringing to man death to sin and life in God.

Our old man is crucified with Him [Jesus], that the body of sin might be destroyed (6:6). If we be dead with Christ, we believe that we shall also live with Him (6:8). For in that he died, he died unto sin once; but in that he [man] lives, he lives unto God (6:10). Therefore, yield yourselves unto God as those who are alive from the dead (6:13).

Flesh still seeks its pleasure, but the mind seeks to serve God; nevertheless, since I am free from the knowledge of good and evil, and delivered from the law of sin and death, there is no condemnation.

There is, therefore, now no condemnation to them who are in Christ Jesus (8:1).

Note very well: Most Bibles add to Romans 8:1 the words "who walk not after the flesh, but after the spirit." These words are *not* in the Greek text! There is absolutely NO condemnation to those in Christ Jesus for they are FREE from the law of sin and death; for they are, in Christ, delivered from the knowledge of good and evil, which was the original sin and the basis of all other so-called sins.

Why? How can this be? Don't we go to church so that we can be taught the difference between good and evil, so that we can shun evil and seek the good? That's what man's doctrines and traditions teach, but that is not what the Bible says. The purpose of gathering together, as given in 1 Corinthians 14:26, is to edify/build up/strengthen one another. Nowhere will you find that the purpose is to condemn one another's behavior.

Why need we not know the difference between good and evil? Because "the law of the Spirit of life in Christ Jesus [Tree of Life] has made me free from the law of sin and death [Tree of Knowledge of Good and Evil]" (Rom. 8:2).

These additional passages from Romans 8 amplify and explain why we need not know the difference between good and evil:

- To be spiritually minded is life and peace (v. 6).
- As many as are led by the Spirit of God, they are the Sons of God (v. 14).
- All things work together for good [that is, all things become or end in good] to them that love God, to them who are the called according to his purpose (v. 28).
- If God is for us, who can be against us (v. 31)?
- Nothing can separate us from the love of God (v. 35–39).

Quite simply, God is Creator; God is all-powerful and sovereign; God is the source of all that is permitted in His creation. Even Satan is nothing more than a tool in the hand of an Almighty God. Hence, there is no good or evil to those in Christ, because the Holy Spirit will convert all that we are and do for God's glory!

God Is Sovereign

"I will call them my people, who were not my people; and will call her beloved, who was not beloved. Those accused of not being my people shall be called the 'Sons of the Living God'" (Rom. 9:25–26).

God's gift to man in Christ Jesus is not a question of human will and human effort, but of God's mercy. It depends not on one's willingness nor on one's own strenuous exertion as in running a race, but on God's having mercy. The Scripture records this message from God to Pharaoh: "I have raised you up for this very purpose of displaying my power in dealing with you, so that My name may be proclaimed the whole world over. So then God has mercy on whomever He wills and He hardens (makes stubborn and unyielding) the heart of whomever He wills (Rom. 9:16–18). (There is no way that man can understand the mystery of God's will, for this would make us arbiters of good and evil.)

Has the potter no right over the clay, to make out of the same lump one vessel for beauty and distinction and honorable use, and another for menial or ignoble and dishonorable use? (Rom. 9:20–23)

Hence, there is nothing, no person, no behavior, no force of opposition that is not a part of God's plan and purpose. If we know not the knowledge of good and evil, we are better off. Then we can perform as God's vessels in whatever way He chooses without our having to make value judgments, because all works together for good in that which God has chosen, for He is the potter and knows the grand scheme and overall plan for the Ages.

Only Believe God!

If you acknowledge and confess with your lips that Jesus is Lord, and in your heart believe that God raised him from the dead, you will be saved (Rom. 10:9)!

No man who believes in Him—who adheres to, relies on and trusts in Him—will ever be put to shame or disappointed (Rom. 10:11).

For everyone who calls upon the name of the Lord shall be saved (Rom. 10:13).

God's Ways Are Not Man's Ways

> Renew your mind. (Rom. 12:2)
> Life = love. (Rom. 13:14–18)

> Judge no one, not even yourself. (Rom. 14:4, 10)
> Nothing is unclean. (Rom. 14:14)
> The Kingdom of God is not external but internal. (Rom. 14:17)

Oh, the depth of the riches both of the wisdom and knowledge of God! How unsearchable are His judgments, and His ways past finding out! For who has known the mind of the Lord? Or, who has been His counselor? For from Him, and through Him, and unto Him are all things: to God be glory forever (Rom. 11:33–36).

Be not conformed to this world, but be transformed by the renewing of your mind (Rom. 12:2).

If your enemy hungers, feed him; if he thirsts, give him drink; for in so doing you shall heap coals of fire on his head (Rom. 12:9–20).[1]

Let us not therefore judge one another anymore (Rom. 14:13).

Happy is the man who condemns not himself in that thing which he allows. In other words, even though God does not condemn you, you will be unhappy if you condemn yourself. Paul also makes the point that, if there is a weaker brother who is still in bondage to the knowledge of good and evil, do not condemn him even for that. You may know there is nothing wrong with what you do, even from God's point of view, but keep it to yourself; don't flaunt your faith in front of others who might be hurt by it (Rom. 14:19–23).

---

1 "Coals of fire" means "burning and purifying love." See Song of Solomon 8:6.

> Note: This is particularly applicable to the book that you are now reading. Reading this book could be injurious to the spiritual health of Christians who have a narrow perspective and/or who have not been filled with, and led by, the Holy Spirit. Before giving copies of this book to a Christian, use your spiritual wisdom to ascertain whether they would be blessed or injured by reading it.

> I know and am persuaded by the Lord Jesus, that there is nothing unclean of itself.
>
> —ROMANS 14:14

> For the Kingdom of God is not food and drink, but righteousness, and peace, and joy in the Holy Spirit.
>
> —ROMANS 14:17

> Now the God of Hope fill you with all joy and peace in believing, that you may abound in Hope, through the power of the Holy Spirit.
>
> —ROMANS 15:13

Glorify God

> Now the God of patience and consolation grant you to be like-minded one toward another according to Christ Jesus, that you may with *one* mind and *one* mouth *glorify God!*
>
> —ROMANS 15:5–6, EMPHASIS ADDED

The Book of Romans concludes with this as its last verse: "To God, only wise, be glory through Jesus Christ forever" (Rom. 16:27).

What a grand and glorious panorama is presented to one whose eye can see and whose ear can hear what the Spirit of the Lord is speaking through Paul's letter to the Romans. In effect, God in Christ Jesus has given man the opportunity to revisit the Garden of Eden, and to begin life anew *without* knowledge of good and evil, *without* law, and, above all, *without* guilt or condemnation! Our sovereign God is using us, one and all, as part of His grand plan for the universe throughout the ages and into eternity. We cannot comprehend, nor necessarily understand, our special role in this, but we can certainly rest in the fact that the role He has ordained for each of us is right. For those who are gay, they can rest in the fact that the condemnation of the gay contained in Romans 1 has been displaced and disposed of in Romans 3–15 for those who have found newness of life in Christ Jesus. For those who are not gay, they may love those who are, as they are, as does their Creator.

Our life, gay or SAD, is from God, in God, and for God—praise God! More than this, we can share with both gay and SAD that God loves each of us just as we are; and He can/will deliver each one from the bondage (the heavy load and complaints) which are inherent in our nature, and which derive from our trying to make it on our own!

That God has a plan is clear from many parts of Scripture. Particularly noteworthy is the Book of Ephesians wherein God's plan for the Church Age, the age in which we are now living, is outlined. In Ephesians 1:4, we note that God had "chosen us in Him [Christ] before the foundation of the world... having predestinated unto the adoption of us as sons by Jesus Christ to Himself." We have already seen in Romans 8 that "sons" are those who are led by the Spirit of God. Hence, we may appear unconventional and out of step with the world, both religious and secular. The important thing, however, is that we not be out of step with the Holy Spirit. We should be willing to hear and to heed what the Spirit of God speaks to our individual hearts.

The narrative in Ephesians proceeds, reaching this crescendo in 1:10–12:

> That in the dispensation of the fullness of times [that is, the last age] He might gather together in One *all things* in

> Christ, both which are in heaven, and which are on earth, even in Him; in whom also we have obtained an inheritance, being predestinated according to the purpose of Him who *works all things after the counsel of His own will* that we should be to the praise of His Glory…

All shall be gathered together in one in Christ—*no exceptions!* Elsewhere it says, "Every knee shall bow and every tongue confess that Jesus Christ is Lord!"

Notice especially in Ephesians 1:11 that we have been "predestinated according to the purpose of Him who works all things after the counsel of His own will." In other words, God has made us a part of His purpose, which is to bring all of His creation into oneness in Christ!

The question, then, must be: "What is God's purpose in creating homosexuals?" Why is homosexuality singled out for special mention ahead of the list of "23" in Romans 1? (Incidentally, 23 + 1 = 24, the number of "heavenly government and worship." Keep this in mind.) And, finally, this question: If being gay is a sin, why has God placed this "unnatural" desire in the hearts of so many of His creatures?

Already, we have indicated that the gay lifestyle is a reflection of the condition of the world, and in some sense, the religious system known as the church at the end of this age.

Confirmation of this opinion comes from consideration of the verbiage used in Romans 1:24–27. As we have seen, one Greek word in particular stands out:

> The men, leaving the natural use of woman, burned in their lust one toward another, men with men, working that which is *unseemly*…
>
> —Romans 1:27

The Greek word *aschemosune,* here translated "unseemly," appears only one other place in the New Testament. That other usage is in Revelation 16 and is clearly associated with the end of the age:

> Behold, I come as a thief. Blessed is he that watches, and keeps his garments, lest he walk naked, and they see his *shame.*
>
> —Revelation 16:15, emphasis added

In looking at the context, we note that Revelation 16 deals with the wrath of God poured out upon those who have the "mark of the beast" (Rev. 16:2). Elsewhere (Rev. 13:17–18) we see the "mark of the beast" defined as the "name" of the beast, or the "number" of his name. This number is given as "666." Since "6" is the number associated with man in his humanity (and, particularly, man who has added to the grace of God [5 + 1] and/or who has missed the Sabbath rest [7 – 1]), the triple "6" (666) seems to signify a perfection of human wisdom.[1] In the subsequent chapter (Rev. 17) we see that the wrath of God is against the "harlot" church—the harlotry of the church being its intercourse with, and acceptance of, the ways of the world while simultaneously claiming to know the differences between good and evil. This is a great mystery, but the harlot is all of the visible church at the end of the age. The harlot is both the "Mother of Harlots" and the daughter harlots (Rev. 17:5). These harlots are the "abomination of the earth," the very same abomination of desolation in consummation spoken of by Daniel and Jesus.

---

[1] Some manuscripts (for example, see footnote to Rev. 13:18 in The Living Bible) give the number here as "616." This could be interpreted as an even stronger reference to Antichrist with the meaning "man as God." Recall that "1" means "primacy" or "beginning" in the sense of "independence or sufficiency that needs no other"—this is a valid description only of God! Sandwiched between two "6s" (recall that two means "witness or testimony" or "opposition or enmity"), "616" would have the meaning "man as God."

Study the depiction of this scarlet-colored beast called the "Mother of Harlots," and know that the "Mother" is the mother church, or Roman Catholicism. The daughter harlots are the great profusion of names (denominations, sects, and assemblies) of blasphemy (17:3), and are all the other "churches" which think they are better than, or different from, Rome (compare to Rev. 3:4). They are all ONE. As it says in Isaiah 1:21–24:

> How is the faithful City [Jerusalem, the church that the Holy Spirit established at Pentecost according to Acts 2] become an Harlot [Babylon the Great]? It was full of justice; righteousness lodged in it, but now murderers [compare to 2 Pet. 2:15–22]. Your silver [grace] has become dross [dull, meaningless, not reflecting the glory of grace], your wine [joy] mixed with water [diluted]. Your princes [priests and pastors] are rebellious, and companions of thieves; everyone loves bribes [generous offerings], and follows after rewards [salaries and other sources of income]; they judge not the fatherless, neither does the cause of the widow come unto them [no mercy].

A harlot is nothing more than a woman who sells her intimacy for money. She (meaning the church) has sold herself to the world. This, then, is the abomination of desolation, which points so clearly to the self-sufficiency of Sodom and Gomorrah wherein mankind sought to place itself beyond the need for God.

What really is the purpose for the church? For believers? Its purpose, their purpose, is to bear fruit. See especially John 15:1–17 wherein Jesus says:

> I am the Vine, you are the Branches. He that abides in Me, and I in him, the same brings forth much fruit; for without Me you can do nothing.

The fruit is defined (John 15:9–14, 17) as "to continue in love." The word *love* is the Greek *agape*, sometimes translated "charity." It is a love that flows outward from the innermost being of a Son of God (one led by the Spirit) and brings life. A somewhat broader definition of "fruit" is found in Galatians 5:22–23:

> The fruit of the Spirit is love, joy, peace, long-suffering, gentleness, goodness, faith, meekness, self-control.

Note that there are nine fruits of the Spirit. The number nine is the number of finality and judgment. It is this "fruit," and this alone, which God desires to see produced in the life of his children/believers.

The absence of this fruit is referred to in 2 Peter 1 as "blindness":

> He that lacks these things is *blind* and cannot see afar off…
>
> —2 Peter 1:9, emphasis added

This is another confirmation that God has raised up the gay community and brought it to daily newspaper, radio and television prominence as a special sign to signify the blindness that pervades mankind (and the institutional church) in this hour.

There is a double meaning, therefore, to the "shame" of nakedness when Christ is revealed. In 1 John it is affirmed that this shame is associated with lack of love. This fruit (love) is produced through intercourse ("knowing") between Christ and a believer. Throughout the Scriptures, in both Old and New Testaments, we see Christ in the male role (groom) and the individual believers, or the church as the corporate believer, in the female role (bride). With the female submitted under the male (see again, John 15:5), much fruit is produced.

The church, however, has departed from this heterosexual relationship and instead has pleasure with its own kind. Regardless of how good it may feel, a homosexual relationship cannot produce offspring (fruit)! And this is, in fact, the great sin of the church at the end of the Church Age.

In Revelation 18 where the fall of Babylon, the Harlot, is described, special mention is made of the fact that:

> The voice of the bridegroom and the bride shall be heard *no more at all* in thee.
>
> —REVELATION 18:23, EMPHASIS ADDED

The church, even true believers, has come to believe a "lie": "...they shall deceive the very elect" (Matt. 24:24; see also 2 Thess. 2:1–12). Simply stated, this "lie" is that men, by working together, can accomplish something for God! But this is false doctrine. Believers, Christians, church members, whatever you want to call them, can together produce nothing, even as the most intimate and prolonged sexual relations among gay men, or among lesbian women, can never produce fruit (children). Yet the great deception is the belief among Christians that such homosexual (man with man) relationships among God's people will produce fruit. Au contraire! Only when the believer, Christian, church member submits, one on one, to the intimacy of a continuing relationship with Jesus Christ can real fruit be produced; and that fruit does constitute new life, for love is the light of life!

In addition to unfruitfulness (especially lack of love), there is at least one additional major weakness in the church (Babylon) at the end of the age. The voice of the bride and groom are no longer heard in her. Not only is this a witness that the former intimacy with Jesus as Lover has disappeared, but it also indicates disintegration of the authority of Jesus as Head of the church.

From 1 Corinthians 11:3, it is evident that there is a divine chain of authority which runs from God the Father to Jesus the Son, to man, to woman. The submission of wife to husband is a special symbol of the submission of the church to Jesus Christ

(Eph. 5:22–25). This is not a popular teaching today in many, if any, churches.

This is the age of women's liberation! But, this too, is a fulfillment of prophecy (Isa. 3:16–4:6). In Revelation 3:14–19, the blind and naked church is called "Laodicea," which literally means "opinions or sayings of the people." The confusion of voices in the visible church, especially those of our women, is no less than in the secular world. Every person thinks he or she is a self-sufficient authority, even concerning spiritual matters. This, in turn, is but another reflection of the digital, or solitary, lifestyle that characterizes much of the gay community.

Why has God brought the gay lifestyle to prominence?

1. God has brought the homosexual to prominence that the whole world, especially including Christendom, both gay and SAD, might symbolically see the fruitlessness of man's wisdom and methods. They have NO spiritual value.

But, there is another reason as well. A harlot is a female who has submitted herself to the intimacy of sexual relations, for money, with someone other than her husband. As we have seen, the whole Book of Revelation damns the "harlot" (the unfaithful church) for literally selling out to the world. In this context, God would rather see the church as a female eunuch. That is, one who can be trusted in the world, as a guardian of the world, without fear that she will become contaminated by intimacy with the world.

I am struck by the fact that, notwithstanding somewhat improved sociological acceptance over the past decade, gay men and women are the true outcasts of society. This sense of being barely tolerated, but not integrated, has been accentuated by the mysterious appearance of AIDS among the gay population at precisely the hour when God is challenging us with one last call to "anoint" our eyes that we may "see" (Rev. 3:18–22). He is calling us who have an "ear" (that is, those who have faith) to "hear" what the Spirit is saying.

2. God has also brought the outcast gays to prominence to challenge a remnant of His people to seek the intimacy of intercourse through "first love" with Him, and not with the world through its harlot church.

Such warning also preceded the first coming of Jesus. Specifically, God had anointed the celibate John the Baptist to preach among sinners in the wilderness, much to the chagrin of the established religious institutions. John was an "outcast" in every sense, as were all who followed Jesus—the so-called "publicans and sinners."

Throughout the Gospel accounts there is counterpoint between Jesus ministering to the outcasts on one side, and the pompous scribes and Pharisees, and Sadduccees on the other side. The present day counterparts of the "scribes and Pharisees" are the so-called evangelical Christians, who have come to place more emphasis on laws (doing good) than on grace; and the present day counterparts of the Sadduccees are the so-called liberal Christians in the "mainline" churches. It is noteworthy that gay men and women are particularly despised by almost everyone, and especially by conservative, evangelical, and/or charismatic Christians.

It should be no surprise, then, if God chooses to repeat history. There is more than one evidence of the cyclical nature of His dealings with His creatures. At the end of the age, before the second coming of Jesus Christ to usher in the next age, the Kingdom Age, we might reasonably expect that God would bypass the established organizations of the visible church, both liberal and conservative, to bring His message of Love and Repentance through the outcasts of society (see again Rom. 9:25–26). There is no more currently prominent, and despised, group of outcasts now alive than homosexuals! Let us each watch and pray, that we might be intimate with our Lord as He moves in His own way in these last days to bring the Church Age to its long awaited and promised conclusion.

Some Concluding Thoughts

For the gay

God loves you as you are! Are you gay only in nature, or is your behavior gay also? Were you born gay (a feminine man or a masculine woman), or are you gay because of the actions of men, in which case you likely are very straight in appearance and manner? What difference does it make? The Lord created you, He loves you, and He seeks an intimate, one-on-one relationship with you. Disregard the opinions and condemnations of men. Know that the man most "despised and rejected of men" (Isa. 53:3) was Jesus.

For the SAD

God loves you as you are! You are what you are by no choice you have made nor by any merit you display, but by the grace of God! Be mindful of one thing only: the Lord created you, has drawn you to Himself, and seeks an intimate one-on-one relationship with you. Judge not others, judge not even yourself, and especially judge not by the opinions of men nor by the standards of the world. Remember that to know and live the truth is a lonely life indeed! (See Romans 3:3–4.)

For both gay and SAD

The message that God has for all of us is this:

1. Whatever you do, do all to the glory of God (1 Cor. 10:31)!

2. As God has distributed [talents, personality, nature] to every man, as the Lord has called everyone, so let him walk (1 Cor. 7:17).

3. Let every person, in whatever state he/she is called by God, there abide with God (1 Cor. 7:24).

These passages from 1 Corinthians are written in connection with a discussion whether one should be married or should remain unmarried. Paul advises that a person is better off unmarried because an unmarried person is "without care/anxiety," because the person that is unmarried "cares for the things that belong to the Lord, how he may please the Lord. But he that is married cares for the things that are of the world, how he may please his wife" (1 Cor. 7:27–33).

On the other hand, Paul says that marriage is nevertheless honorable, and, of course, that it exemplifies the relationship between Christ and the church.

The bottom line is this: *Let every person in whatever situation or condition he or she was in when God called them to become a Christian, rest there at peace and in contentment until the situation or condition is changed by God.*

If you are gay, be content: none but God can change you. If you are not gay, be content; there are none that you can change. Open your eyes and see God—see not just His acts, but understand His ways (His mind). (Compare to Psalm 103:7.)

In seeing God as Creator, and, more than this, as a Creator who loves all of His creation, we can begin to love Him. As we love Him, we come to know Him:

> If any man love God, the same is known of him.
>
> —1 Corinthians 8:3

"Knowing God" is to be intimate with Him. Being intimate will produce fruit, and will release even more of His life and love into our lives, resulting in more praise, and more life and more love, until we are totally transformed one day into His likeness and image, which was His original purpose in creation. "Let us make man in our image, after our likeness" (Gen. 1:26).

This is more than fanciful doctrine. In 1970 a book entitled *Prison to Praise* by Merlin Carothers was published to document miracles that occurred in response to praise.[2] In the most unbelievable, depressing situations, Carothers would counsel the persons involved to thank and praise God for the depressing situation. These situations ranged from fear, loneliness, rejection, and betrayal by a loved one, to depression, hunger, and fear of death. I myself have so counseled individuals, and have seen that, as the person "gives up" and surrenders—in effect, abandons human thought and logic—the love of God becomes totally sufficient and miraculously changes the circumstance from negative to positive.

Essentially, to give praise to God amounts to no more than accepting ourselves as we are, as God accepts us, and praising Him for the inner joy and peace He has given us in Jesus Christ. Through praise, we rest in God, at peace, knowing that we cannot change, nor transform, our desires of the flesh nor the circumstances and situations which surround us. However, as we praise and glorify His name, we are overtly acknowledging that God is in control and that He can effect these changes, whether in our nature, our behavior, or in our external circumstances associated with where we live and work, or don't work, or even our relationships with friends and relatives. In short, we acknowledge that we, as individuals, are insufficient, human relationships and methods are insufficient, and that God is all sufficient. That is the truth implicit in the story of Sodom and Gomorrah. The Lord would have us see and receive this truth as the Key to unlocking the door of fellowship with Him in these dark closing hours of the present age.

Praise God! He created the world, and He has not abandoned His creation. He loves and cares for us, and desires that each one of us become one with Him. In becoming one with Him, we become one with each other. *But, the sequence cannot be reversed!*

If the sin of Sodom and Gomorrah was the "heaviness" of self-sufficiency, then Isaiah 61:3 confirms the solution: "...the garment of praise [lifts] the spirit of heaviness."

It is no wonder, then, that in Revelation, wherein the "heaviness" of the church at the end of the age is depicted in such graphic and depressing detail, we find also so many references to acts of praise and worship. For example:

> And they sing the song of Moses, the servant of God, and the song of the Lamb, saying, "Great and Marvelous are your works, Lord God Almighty; just and true are your ways, O King of Saints."
>
> —REVELATION 15:3

> You are worthy, O Lord, to receive glory and honor and power; for you have created all things, and for your pleasure they are and were created.
>
> —REVELATION 4:11

Whoever you are, God created you for Himself. He desires an intimate and personal relationship with each of us. Rejoice in Him, knowing that He knows you, and that you are a part of His eternal plan and purpose. Praise the Lord!

What Are God's People to Do?

Abortion—parents murdering their own children—the church choking, suffocating and killing its children (i.e., the children of the Kingdom, the children of God) by placing them in bondage to the knowledge of good and evil, treating them as chattel or merchandise, and driving them back into the world.

Homosexuality—love of man for his own gender in sexual relationships which produce no fruit/no offspring—the voices of the Bridegroom (the Lord Jesus) and of the bride (the one who loves and submits to Him) are no more heard.

Are abortion and homosexuality sins to be punished? No more so than any other sin, whether pride or boasting, gossiping, or disobedience to parents (Rom. 1:24–32). God would have us ignorant of these things, knowing not the difference between good and evil, but rather walking as children led by His Spirit.

What is the condition of the church? How can I characterize the lukewarmness in my own heart? In a word, we have left our "first love" (Rev. 2:4). More than this, we don't even know what love is!

God is love! If we know not love, we know not God (Rom. 8:3; 1 John 4:8)!

Recall that, toward the conclusion of our discussion of abortion, we looked at 2 Peter 2:20–21, where the children turn away from the "holy commandment" delivered to them. Jesus has given us only two commandments:

> Love the Lord your God with all your heart.
>
> Love your neighbor as yourself.

There are two aspects to loving our neighbor. Jesus "loved the world" and gave Himself for it. This concept is embodied in the King James translation of love/agape, which is "charity." But this love for the world is totally different from the love that Christians should have for one another.

Our love for one another is embodied in the deeper meaning of love/agape, which is to become "one." Hence, Jesus prayed at Gethsemane that we "*may be one,* as you, Father, are in me, and I in you, that *they also may be one in us*; that the world may believe that you have sent me" (John 17:21, emphasis added).

In the 1970s, during that great outpouring of the Holy Spirit, we sang of our oneness in the Spirit.

Have you sung it recently? Why is it out of vogue? The world will be drawn to Christ when we love the Lord Jesus (our husband) with all of our heart (giving up our homosexual lifestyle) and when our love for each other makes us one (because we are one in Christ) (thereby no longer murdering God's children) wherein we produce and nurture "children of God" who grow up to become "sons of God.

Unless we love as God loves, we cannot know God, nor His ways, nor will the world be drawn to us like bees to honey. Yet, this is God's plan and purpose for us—to know Him and to know His ways. (Compare to Psalm 103:7; there is a difference between seeing God's acts and knowing His ways!) When we love, know love, and see love, as God is Love, our understanding of God's creation, purpose and redemptive plan for the ages will overwhelm us with its majesty and His glory.

God's objective and purpose is a "new creation"—a new order of things wherein God will be "all in all" (1 Cor. 15:28). This creation had its beginning in the first man to achieve Sonship (the faithful and true witness of Rev. 3:14). In Christ we are a part of this new creation (2 Cor. 5:17). This "new creation" is a work of reconciliation wherein the world will become one with God. (Compare to 2 Corinthians 5:19.)

Although we frequently refer to Jesus as the Christ ("the anointed one"), in fact the Christ is a corporate being of which Jesus is the Head, and of which we, as sons, shall comprise the body (Eph. 1:21–23). Note from Ephesians 1:23 that the "body" is the fullness of Him that fills all in all—in other words, full of and led by the Holy Spirit.

The product of this third massacre of babies, this age of abortion, shall be the Christ—the anointed one—the perfect man. Christ as a corporate being is best exemplified by the picture in Psalm 133:2:

> Behold, how good and how pleasant it is for brethren to dwell together in unity! It is like the precious ointment upon the head, that ran down upon the beard, even Aaron's beard; that went down to the skirts of his garments.

The corporate Christ consists of Jesus "the head over all things to the church, which is His body, the fullness of Him that fills all in all" (Eph. 1:22–23; 4:15–16; Col. 1:18–19). In fact, Ephesians 1:17–23 comprises a prayer by Paul that we might receive this "revelation" of the Christ by having the eyes of our understanding enlightened.

While Jesus was on earth, He was also Christ—there was only the Head—but the Head now has an ever-growing body which by travail of the saints shall give birth to the company who shall stand in Zion with the Lamb.

What are Christians to do in this age of abortion and homosexuality? We are to travail. John 17, which has been called Jesus' High Priestly, Intercessory Prayer, pictures for us the function of believers at the golden altar. Note that the context of this intercession is that "the world has been overcome" (John 16:33). Life eternal is seen not to be time related, but life is the increasing knowledge of the true God (John 17:3). This we would expect, for in this realm we are in His presence.

Can you and I become the "I" in Chapter 17? This is the intention and purpose to which we are called (vv. 18, 22–24). It is for *now,* if we would enter in. Do not rationalize away Jesus' words as in some measure "future-spective." We do ourselves a disservice if we doubt that Jesus meant what he said. He said:

> And *now I am* no more in the world...
>
> —John 17:11, emphasis added

> Father, I will that they also, whom you have given me, *be with Me where I am,* that they may behold My glory...
>
> —John 17:24, emphasis added

Fellow Christians, all the symbolism of the tabernacle has been fulfilled except for the golden altar which is at the threshold between the place of worship and the place where God dwells in His glory. In the charismatic revival we had fulfilled the table of shewbread, a place of fellowship and renewal. At the golden altar we come, at least figuratively, alone, as intercessors, pleading for the deliverance of God's creation from bondage.

This is a hidden work—hidden from the eyes of men. It is a work of true agape love, for there is no earthly reward for that which is done in secret.

For confirmation, let us recall again that we live in the age of, and are a part of the church of, Laodicea. The admonitions which the Lord gives us who live in this age conclude with "Open the door" and "Be an overcomer" (Rev. 3:20–21).

The first usage of *door* (Matt. 6:6) relates to praying in secret. The second usage of *door* (Matt. 25:10) refers to identification with the bridegroom and entering into the marriage relationship. The third and fourth usages refer to the closing of the sepulcher (grave-site) after Jesus was dead and buried (Matt. 27:60), but from which he emerged triumphant over death (and the flesh and the world) (Matt. 28:2)! The fifth usage (Mark 1:33) specifically describes petition by "all the city gathered at the door."

In comparing Revelation 3:7–8 with 3:20, it is clear that the petitioning man (who is part of the body of overcomers who constitute the spiritual city of Jerusalem) has authority to open the door which separates him from the presence of the glory of God. He opens it with the "key of David"! There is much speculation about the significance of this "key," but the simplest explanation is usually correct. Recall that "David" means "beloved," and it was this "beloved" upon whom the Spirit of the Lord rested (1 Sam. 16:13). He was a "man after God's own heart who shall fulfill all my will" (1 Sam. 13:14; Acts 13:22). David was a builder/edifier who was destined to "build a house for my name, and I will establish the throne of his Kingdom forever" (2 Sam. 7:13).

Dwelling in love and being led of God's Spirit, thereby doing His will, is the basis for opening "the door" which stands between the Lord and us. On one side we stand as petitioners, and on the other side dwells the presence and glory of God.

Immediately upon the door being opened, Revelation 4:1 speaks of the presence of the Lord and his purpose in creation being revealed.

Similarly, we could trace "overcome" through the New Testament. The first usage (Luke 11:22) clearly denotes that "to overcome" involves strength and will. In the second usage (John 16:33), Jesus sets the example of overcoming (2 is the number of witness) by acknowledging, or promising, that we shall experience trouble/tribulation in the world, but that we can nevertheless be of good cheer, for he has overcome the world; and, so can we!

To overcome (third usage; Rom. 3:3–4) is to depend upon the faithfulness of God, knowing that his truth shall abound despite all the lies in the world; and that, in Christ, we shall be judged righteous.

In Revelation alone there are seventeen usages of "overcome," of which 10 relate to the responsibility of believing Christians. The last usage (27th) asserts that "He that overcomes shall inherit all things, and I will be his God, and he shall be My son" (Rev. 21:7). The alternative is the "second death," which is second life (compare to Gen. 2:17) in the lake of purifying fire.

Hence, the challenge for believing Christians is to transcend the opinions/untruths/errors which comprise the teachings/sayings of the Laodicean Church Age, and to see God as He really is—and to partake of His nature—which nature is radiant, contagious love:

> God is love. God is light. God is holy.

These are the only "God is" statements in the New Testament. One can conclude, therefore, that:

> Love = Light = Holy[1]

---

[1] *Holy* means "set apart unto God."

One can only see if there is true light. The only true light that shines is the radiance of the glory of God which is love. This love is not to be flaunted, or profaned, in the world, nor should it be confused with the brotherly love of Philadelphia, but rather it is essentially a secret, or sacred, ministry of intercession before the veil/door which separates us from the throne room of the Living God.

We know that this veil/door is the flesh (Heb. 10:20). More specifically, the veil represents ignorance, dishonesty, walking in craftiness, and handling the word of God deceitfully. But when with unveiled face we behold the glory of the Lord, "we are changed into that same image, from glory to glory," by the Spirit of the Lord (2 Cor. 3:14–4:6). This change, or transfiguration, comes from seeing the presence of the Lord—and this comes only by the light of Love in the holy place (at the golden altar of priestly ministry on behalf of God's people) (1 John 3:8; Eph. 3:17–19; 1 Cor. 8:3).

The golden altar ministry is specifically portrayed and described by the experience of Zacharias, who prayed in the holy place for a "son" (compare to John 16–17 and Rev. 12:5, 13, which describe the birth of the corporate Son, the Christ with both glorified Head and body).

When the angel Gabriel announced to Zacharias that His prayer for a "son" would be answered, Zacharias, who had petitioned in prayer, doubted. He doubted the possibility of the fulfillment of his own request! He was struck dumb!

In short, Zacharias' flesh had prevented him from entering into and seeing the glory of God. When the son was born, Zacharias testified to the Love of God, and his mouth was opened, and he "spoke and praised God" giving testimony to His love and mercy, and then went on to describe God's redemptive purpose and plan in creation to bring light (love) and peace among His people (Luke 1:64–80).

May we seek to do the hidden work, going beyond the "fellowship in the gospel" (Phil. 1:5), and beyond the "fellowship of the

Spirit" (Phil. 2:1), to "know Him, and the power of His resurrection (passing through the closed door) and the "fellowship of his sufferings" (Phil. 3:10). "Suffering" is Love. Love endures all things, and never fails. Love is as absolute as death (Song of Sol. 8:6), and provides a new dimension of sight, so that we no longer see the world, but come "face to face" with the glory of the Lord "to know Him fully even as I am fully known" (1 Cor. 13:4–12)!

God is sending a message to His church in the form of spiritual parables—such as abortion and homosexuality. May we heed these parables and turn from the bondage of the knowledge of good and evil, and from the praiseworthy methods of man to secret pleading before our God for the conclusion of His great work of Love. Let us intercede before the throne for the great culmination of God's purpose:

1. He shall dwell in the midst of His people (Rev. 21:3).

2. There shall be the death of death (Rev. 21:4; 1 Cor. 15:26).

3. God shall be "all in all" (1 Cor. 15:28).

2 — In the Heavenlies

Question: *Why do we meet on Sunday morning? What purpose or benefit is there to meeting as a group, whether 10, 100, or 1,000 gather together? What is the church?*

I believe these questions have gone through many of our minds. I would like to share with you some insight the Lord has given to enable us to distinguish the church as God sees it. To begin with, it is important to emphasize that there is no merit in any particular meeting. There is not even any merit in the particular group of individuals that God has allowed to gather. And yet, in another sense, He has chosen each group carefully to let us see in microcosm the way that God sees the whole church. In other words, if all of the church is somehow represented in the midst of our group, then we have a vision, in a small way, of what God sees when he sees the church.

The first thing we should see in the Scripture is that the church is like a city. When we think about a city, we think about a group of people who are closely allied with one another. They live and work together. They are interlocked and interdependent. When Babylon, the first city, was invented, if I may use that expression, its founder Nimrod became very famous. As a matter of fact, a whole religious structure, the religious structure that we know today, grew up around Nimrod because he founded the first city and people were grateful. Essentially, what that first city did was to put walls around the people. The city kept the people safe from wild, vicious animals and marauding tribes who would prey upon the people. The city brought security, and that is what is at the core of what a city is all about. A city brings security!

The names of two cities are mentioned prominently in the Scriptures: Babylon, the very first city; and Jerusalem, the city of God. These cities are important to us because both are used in the Scriptures to represent or describe the church. Both are looked to by men as a source of spiritual security. But only one provides a true security; the other is false.

The city of Babylon is the church as the world has made it, and it is an abomination in the sight of God. Jerusalem is the church as God would see it, and it is a thing of beauty in the eyes of God. The mystery is how, in some measure, the same person can be in both these different cities. But it is clear that we are admonished throughout the Word to "Come out of her, my people"[1]—Come out of the city of Babylon and live wholly and exclusively in the city of Jerusalem, which is the city of God.

Many times people will say, How can I know what God is saying in His Word? How can I know in what measure the Catholics, Lutherans, Presbyterians, Methodists, Baptists, Nazarenes, Pentecostals, or Charismatics, or whatever, are wrong or right? How do I know what is God's truth? The answer is found in an understanding of these two cities and especially of the differences between them. You will recall that Babylon was a city that man built, reaching up to heaven. It is a city that is rooted in the earth, a city whose foundations are earthly (or fleshly). It is man reaching up to God that he may be righteous in his own sight. You recall what God did—he looked at this city building a tower toward heaven. It was an abomination in his sight. He confused their languages and scattered the people. If we go back into that account in Genesis 11, we see that

[1] Go forth from Babylon… Flee out of the midst of Babylon, and deliver every man his soul… My people, go out of the midst of her… Deliver thyself, O Zion, that dwells with the daughter of Babylon… Come out of her, my peoples… (Isaiah 48:20; Jeremiah 50:8, 51:6, 51:45; Zechariah 2:7; Revelation 18:4)

the very reason they built this tower was that they might have a "name," a name in the world. God didn't want them known by that name. He wanted them known by His name.

The word *babel* is derived from Babylon. A babel is a confusion of voices where you hear everyone talking at once, and yet you don't hear anyone really. That is what the word *Babylon* means—it means "confusion."

That is what we have in the church today; we have confusion. Confusion comes not from God, but from man. Man has modeled the church and his interpretations of Scripture after his own earthbound and evil (selfish) heart. Man builds his doctrines, puts his name, or a name, on them, and defends them to the death because of his pride, which is both the original sin and the sin of Babylon. As a result, man has built an institution, which he calls the church, into many organizations, each of which reflects his own personal desires, his own views, and exalts man. Look at the churches around you. You will see a steeple on most of them, even if a tiny one, as a symbol of man reaching up to heaven. And you will see inscribed across the front of it the name of a man, or a name that stands for a man. Below that name you will see on almost every church the name of a pastor. This is an institution that exalts man, and it breeds confusion.

On the other hand, we find in the Book of Revelation that Jerusalem is not a city that has been raised up in the earth, but that comes down from heaven. The word *Jerusalem* means "founded upon peace." Another word we could use as a synonym might be *order,* the opposite of Babylon. In Babylon is confusion. Everyone is clamoring to be heard. In Jerusalem there is an order, a unity, a oneness. There is a central focus and that is Jesus. Paul talks about it in Ephesians 4: "One body, and one Spirit, even as ye are called in one hope of your calling; one Lord, one faith, one baptism, one God and Father of all, who is above all, and through all, and in you all." There is unity. There is only one truth. It is revealed to us by the Holy Spirit as we yield ourselves to Him without preconceptions or mental reservations.

Jerusalem contrasts with Babylon even in the matter of languages. At Pentecost, when the New Jerusalem came into being, there were many languages spoken, but they were heard not as a confusing babble, but with a single understanding—they heard praise to God! This contrast is sharp and clear. We dare not disregard it, but must seek spiritual discernment to distinguish Jerusalem from Babylon.

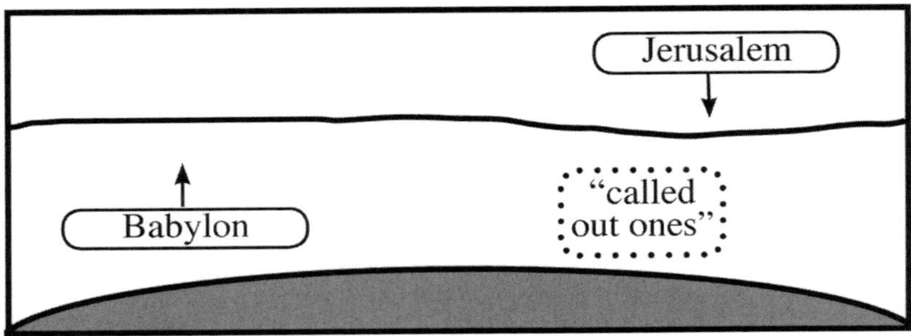

This diagram illustrates that, in terms of the scriptural expressions of the church as a city, there is no church on the ground, in the earth. If we have the New Jerusalem in the heavenlies, and the Babylon outfit is on the earth, but this isn't of God, then what is of God? How do we know whether we are part of Babylon? This is where the word *church* itself (Greek: *ekklesia*) comes in. *Church* means "called out." It means "a body of people who are not rooted in the earth." They are called out of the earthly realm to live quite literally in the heavenly realm ("the heavenlies").

Turn to Ephesians, the book of the church. (If we want to see the church as God sees it, if we want to understand the church as God knows it, then we need to study Ephesians carefully.) Now—very basic and fundamental to God's understanding and perspective on the church are these words found in Ephesians 1:3, 10 (emphasis added):

> Blessed be the God and Father of our Lord Jesus Christ, who has blessed us with all spiritual blessings *in the heavenlies* ["in heavenly places"] in Christ...that in the dispensation of the fullness of times he might gather together in one all things in Christ, both which are in heaven, and which are on earth, in Him.

Where are your blessings? Where are my blessings? Where are the blessings of every Christian? In the heavenlies! That's where your blessings are. Church, your blessings are *not* on this earth, and they are not earthly. We have been called out of this world, away from this earth.

If we read John 17 carefully, we see that Jesus said that those who are "called" are "in the world, but not of the world." We are physically present in the world, but we don't belong here. The reason that we are not of it is that our blessings are not here! Our blessings are in the heavenlies! People ("Antichrist") might make fun of this truth by saying that we are concerned with "pie in the sky by-and-by." But that is not what we have just said. The Lord wants us to see that right *today* we are blessed in Christ and these blessings are in the heavenlies. In order for us to appropriate, or take advantage of, these blessings, we must see into the heavenlies. We must see where we are.

One of the reasons for error in the church is that we are earthbound, and we insist on interpreting God's Word at the natural or earthly level.

As another background element, let's compare Zechariah 6:12 with Philippians 3:20. First, we need to say a word about "the Branch." Most readers just accept that the Branch is Jesus. For some time, in my spirit, I have felt that this was wrong, that the Branch is not Jesus, but that it refers to Christ. What's the difference? Jesus (Jah Saves) is God as Savior, the Son of

God. Christ (anointed one) is God as the anointed Son of Man, and includes all of us in Him. The Branch, therefore, is not just Jesus, but is Jesus with His saints; it is Jesus as the Christ, the Son of Man, of which he is the Head and we are the body. (Compare Ephesians 1:22-23, "... And gave him to be the head over all to the church, which is His body, the fullness of Him that filleth all in all.")

> Behold, the man whose name is THE BRANCH, and *he shall grow up out of his place,* and he shall build the temple of the LORD: Even he shall build the temple of the LORD; and he shall bear the glory, and shall sit and rule upon his throne; and he shall be a priest upon his throne: and the counsel of peace shall be between them both.
>
> —ZECHARIAH 6:12–13, EMPHASIS ADDED

The significant thing is that the Branch, which includes you and me, grows up "out of his place"—that means we are growing up in a place we do not belong.

> For our citizenship is in heaven, from where also we look for the Savior, the Lord Jesus Christ.
>
> —PHILIPPIANS 3:20

Our citizenship is in heaven, but we are growing up out of our place. We are growing up in the world, but this is not our place. Our place is in the heavenlies. It is just as if my family and I were living in France, even though we remained American citizens. My children would be growing up out of their place. We would live by French laws, attend French schools, eat French food, live in a French house, drive a French car, and even speak French, but we would not be French. We would be Americans growing up out of our place.

That's what the Scriptures are telling us here about God's purpose for the church. The church dare not see this world as its place. Remember this, for you are going to hear more and more in Christian circles (as we move along toward End Times) of the responsibility of Christians to clean up the world and to make it a better place to live.[1] Even the elect shall be deceived—Matthew 24:24. Compare especially 2 Thessalonians 2:1–12, verse 4—"exalteth himself" and "sitteth in the temple of God.") *But our blessings are not in this world!* They are in the heavenlies! We are here in this world, and we should pray for it and for its rulers, but our position and our blessings are in the heavenlies. The blessings are received only insofar as we acknowledge that *we are called out*. Praise God!

What we should see as the difference between one gathering of believers and another gathering in some different place is that there is less likelihood, where there are not a lot of programs and organizations and systems, that one will see the meeting (the church organization) as an end in itself. This is the tragedy—that we see meetings as ends in themselves. Any of us can fall into this trap. If you see any Christian gathering or Bible study, whether inside or outside of a church building, as an end in itself (by that I mean that you see merit in just attending), you are in Babylon, and may as well be in a cold and desolate cathedral.

The significance of this is that, in the final analysis, all that we are in a spiritual sense is individual and personal. There is no such thing as a corporate citizenship. We are individual citizens of the heavenly Kingdom, the Kingdom of God. As individuals we may receive ministry at a meeting or gathering of believers for our spiritual good, but the meeting in and of itself as an end has no spiritual merit or value. We each need to see that. If we do not see it, we are in Babylon.

Now, if our blessings are in the heavenlies (glory to God!)...This is an exciting word. Even if you do not totally

---

[1] This sentence was written in the late 1970s!

understand or receive all that is being said here, you should soak it up and remember these words because one day God will reveal its full meaning to you! If our blessings are in the heavenlies, what can we know of the heavenlies? There are several things we can know of the heavenlies.

Note from this diagram: we are on the earth, and the heavens are above us. The first and most obvious thing we know is found in Psalm 103:11:

> The heavens are high above the earth.

One of the surprises we find in studying the "heavens" or "heavenlies," is that the same word for heaven, both in the Hebrew[1] and in the Greek,[2] is used to refer to both the natural or physical heavens which we can see with our eyes and also the spiritual heavens in which God dwells. This fact has been a source of confusion to many. But, if we see as God sees, we will see there is no difference. In God's eyes there is no difference between the physical (or natural) and the spiritual. It is all one in God's sight. But, in either case, the first thing we need to realize is that the heavenlies are "high above the earth." The more we get into Christ, the farther away we're going to get from this earth, and the less meaning earth will have for us, the less value it will have for us, the less merit we will see in it and the rewards it offers. The ultimate goal for the Christian should be, as the expression frequently used in derision says, to "become so heavenly minded that we're no earthly good." I will praise God when we reach that day.

In John 17 where Jesus is clearly seen in the heavenlies, even though he is still physically or geographically on this earth, in verse 1 it says:

> Jesus...lifted His eyes to heaven.

Now, what are we to understand by that? Look carefully at the context:

> These words spoke Jesus, and [then] lifted up His eyes to heaven...

What words had he just spoken? In John 16:33, just preceding, his words are recorded:

> I have overcome the world.

The heavenlies (heaven) and the world are incompatible and separated by a gulf. The more we overcome of the world, the more we begin to see of heaven. Praise God!

We need to see heaven as God sees it. In Amos 9:6 we read:

> And the Lord God of Hosts is he who builds his stories [chambers] in the heavens...

"Builds stories"—as in first story, second story, third story, referring to levels or floors. The Hebrew word translated here "stories" or "chambers" is translated in most other places in either of two ways: "stairs," or "degrees." For example, there is a series of Psalms called "Songs of Degrees." This is the same Hebrew word. This verse in Amos tells us that the heavenlies are built in degrees, or stories, like levels or floors.

Parenthetically, let us look at 2 Corinthians 5:1–2, 5:

> We have a building of God, an house not made with hands, eternal in the heavens. For in this we groan, earnestly desiring to be clothed upon with our house which is from heaven ...Now He that hath wrought us for the very same thing is God.

God wants and intends for us to be clothed with the fullness of heaven. Do we have to die in the body to realize God's intention? Not at all, for in the last day some shall be transfigured directly. Also, let us be careful to distinguish the spirit, soul, and body. The former may be clothed before the latter.

How many stories does heaven have? "Three" is the number spoken of and represented in Scripture. There are three heavens, or three chambers in the heavenlies, at least those which concern us. (Compare to 2 Corinthians 12:2, "caught up to the third heaven.") You will also recall that "1" is the number of beginnings, "2" the number of witness or separation, and "3" the number of divine perfection.

There is a principle of scriptural interpretation that reflects the "alpha and omega," the beginning and the ending. If you want an interesting and different way to study the Bible, look for the first and last. (For example, the Old Testament begins with "God" and ends with "curse"; the New Testament begins with "Christ" and ends with "grace." Another good example is that Romans opens with a prayer (1:11) that we might be "established" and closes (16:25–26) with the fact that to be established involves "the obedience of faith.") With respect to our present study, let's look at the first and last verses of Ezekiel.

> The heavens were opened, and I saw visions of God.
>
> —EZEKIEL 1:1

The "heavens were opened." We see then that the heavens, or heavenlies, can be opened! They can be opened, and we can see into heaven! Now look at the last verse of Ezekiel (48:35):

> And the name of the city from that day shall be, the Lord [Jehovah] is there.

This summarizes all that Ezekiel saw in the opened heavens. He saw the New Jerusalem. He saw the presence of the Lord. When the heavens are opened, there is the Lord (Jehovah). Jehovah, the I AM, is in heaven.

> The heavens were opened unto him, and he saw the Spirit of God descending…
>
> —Matthew 3:16 (see also Mark 1:10; Luke 3:21)

The heavens opened. The Holy Spirit descended. The Holy Spirit is in heaven.

> But he [Stephen], being *full of the Holy Spirit, looked up steadfastly* into heaven, and saw the glory of God, and Jesus standing on the right hand of God, and said, behold, I see the *heavens opened*, and the Son of Man standing on the right hand of God.
>
> —Acts 7:55–56, emphasis added

He looked up into heaven (his eyes were no longer on earthly things), and he saw the glory, the presence of God, the Son of Man standing. (Compare John 1:47, "no guile," and John 1:51, "Ye shall see heaven open, and…the Son of Man.") Stephen saw Jesus and the Son of Man (the Christ) standing on the right hand of God; he had to be "full of the Spirit" to see. In the heavens we see God, his throne (Ps. 103:19; Isa. 66:1; Matt. 5:34), his Spirit, and Jesus the Christ standing. I believe He stands through all the heavens.

In Ezekiel 43:10, it is recorded that God spoke to Ezekiel with a voice of judgment against the church, for Israel represents the church. He said, in effect, "You need to measure the church."

And He tells Ezekiel how to measure.

> Show the house to the house of Israel, that they may be ashamed of their iniquities; let them measure the pattern... That they may keep the whole form of it, and all its ordinances, and do them.
>
> —EZEKIEL 43:10–11

Ezekiel was shown a pattern in the heavenlies that he was to share with the church, with Israel. We know from Exodus 25 that Moses also was shown the "pattern" for the tabernacle in the heavenlies. This is described in Hebrews 8:1–5 (emphasis added):

> Now of the things which we have spoken this is the sum: we have such an high priest, who is seated on the right hand of the throne of the majesty in the heavens, a minister of the sanctuary, and of *the true tabernacle*, which the Lord pitched, and not man... (every earthly levitical priest) serve unto the example and shadow of heavenly things, as Moses was admonished of God when he was about to make the tabernacle; for, see, saith he, that thou make all things according to the *pattern* shown to thee in the mount.

The true tabernacle is in heaven! The tabernacle of Moses, therefore, reflects what we see in heaven when heaven is opened.

> For Christ is not entered into the holy places made with hands, which are the *figures of the true*, but into heaven itself, now to appear in the presence of God for us.
>
> —HEBREWS 9:24

Heaven is what we see in the tabernacle! Of course, as you know, in the tabernacle we see three compartments: the outer court, the holy place, and the holiest of all, or holy of holies—1, 2, 3!

3. Divine Perfection	HOLY OF HOLIES	Abode of God
2. Witness/Separation	HOLY PLACE	Stars
1. Beginning	OUTER COURT	Clouds

There are three stories, or degrees, or compartments in the heavenlies. Many folks (for example, the notes in my Scofield Bible) interpret these three heavens as "the clouds," "the stars," and "the place of God's abode." At first, I reacted against these notes as unspiritual, but the Lord was gracious to allow me to see that these characterizations are correct. But, we must see that they are correct not just in a physical sense, but also in a spiritual sense! We will come back to this.

Everything we have shared to this point has been an introduction. Our objective is to look into the heavens. There is a very real sense in which we can be, *now*, in these three heavens. This is God's will and purpose for us. The purpose of the church, in terms of edifying and helping one another, is to help each of us to climb these stairs, or to progress through the degrees, thereby moving through the first heaven, and through the second heaven, and into the fullest experience of the manifest presence of God in the third heaven.

What is the first heaven? The most obvious description is that it is like the outer court of the tabernacle, and it's like the clouds. In other words, it is the most visible and most accessible part of heaven. Let's do a quick study of "clouds" in the New Testament. There are twenty-five places where the word "clouds" is used. The primary themes associated with its usage are:

The Coming Christ	Matt. 24:30; 26:64; Mark 13:26; 14:62; Luke 12:54; 21:27; Rev. 1:7
Transfiguration (Establishment of the Kingdom)	Matt. 17:5; Mark 9:7; Luke 9:34–35
Ascension	Acts 1:9; 1 Thess. 4:17
Identification	1 Cor. 10:1–2

Each of these themes has to do with "beginnings" and with the visible. Especially significant is the concept of identification in 1 Corinthians 10. Most obvious, of course, is the "coming" Christ, which for now we will leave for the Spirit to reveal.

To further aid our understanding, let us consider another parenthesis, or two. In the Gospel of John, Chapter 1, there are five days spoken of. Because the Spirit invites special attention to the sequence of these five days, there is great spiritual meaning here. In fact, we receive here understanding of the spiritual progression involved with coming to Jesus and in advancing through the heavenlies.

Day one

> John bore witness of Him [Jesus].
>
> —John 1:15

This day is not counted as relates to the heavenlies—this represents the natural or earth realm when we hear about Jesus, and before we have come to Him. In fact, this day is the only one of the five not explicitly denoted. In a sense it is before spiritual time ("born again") has commenced."

Day two

> The next day…John *sees Jesus coming*…Behold, the Lamb of God who takes away the sin of the world [salvation].
>
> —JOHN 1:29

This equates to the first heavenly realm, the realm of spiritual beginnings, the outer court wherein is salvation; i.e., justification by faith.

Day three

> Again the next day…
>
> —JOHN 1:35

> They *followed Jesus.*
>
> —JOHN 1:37

> Where do you dwell?
>
> —JOHN 1:38

> *Come and see.*
>
> —JOHN 1:39

This equates to the second heaven, the following and seeking realm.

Day four

> The day following…
>
> —JOHN 1:43

> Behold, an Israelite indeed, in whom is *no guile.*
>
> —JOHN 1:47

> Thou *shalt see*…
>
> —JOHN 1:50

> Ye shall see *heaven open*, and the messengers of God ascending and descending upon the Son of Man [the Christ].
>
> —John 1:51

This equates to the third heaven, through the veil which is our flesh, where we no longer see as through a glass darkly, but see Him face to face. This is to be and to know the Son of Man in His fullness.

Day five

> And the third day...there was a marriage.
>
> —John 2:1

> Both Jesus was called, and his disciples, to the marriage.
>
> —John 2:2

The identification of this fifth day as the third day hints at a double dimension; i.e., temporal as well as spatial progression. The entrance into the holiest involves an ascension and a consummation. Compare to Revelation 19:1, "After these things" and Revelation 19:7, "For the marriage of the Lamb is come, and His wife hath made herself ready." Compare also to John 4:34, "My food is to do the will of Him that sent me and to finish His work." The wedding shall occur when heaven is manifested on earth—"Thy Kingdom come, on earth, as it is in heaven."

A second parenthesis which I should like to share with you has to do with a puzzling verse which, it turns out, confirms our understanding of the heavenlies. This "key" verse is found in Matthew 7:7–8 and Luke 11:9–10. This is a very simple and well known scripture. It has been a puzzle for me because the meaning of its apparent redundancy has not for me, until recently, been evident.

> Ask, and it shall be given you; seek, and ye shall find; knock, and it shall be opened unto you. For everyone that

> asketh, receiveth; and he that seeketh findeth; and to him that knocketh it shall be opened.
>
> —MATTHEW 7:7–8

The puzzling aspect of this verse has always been—Why is the same thing said in three different ways? And, why, if there is significance to the three-fold redundancy, do the three different expressions occur in this order?

1. Ask—and it shall be given you (verb in passive voice)
2. Seek—and ye shall find (verb in active voice)
3. Knock—and it shall be opened unto you (verb passive)

There is a very simple way to study the Word of God. We can just take these three words—ask, seek, knock—and, using a concordance, find what is associated with each as they are used in Scripture. Following are many of the expressions associated with "ask," which we will see clearly is associated with the first heaven:

> Your Father knows what things ye have need of, before ye ask Him.
>
> —MATTHEW 6:8

> Ask bread.
>
> —MATTHEW 7:9

> Ask a fish.
>
> —MATTHEW 7:10

> Your Father who is in heaven [knows how to] give good things to them that ask Him.
>
> —MATTHEW 7:10

If two shall agree on earth as touching anything that they shall ask, it shall be done.

—MATTHEW 18:19

Desiring a certain thing of Him...But Jesus answered and said, Ye know not what ye ask.

—MATTHEW 20:20, 22

And all things, whatever ye shall ask in prayer...

—MATTHEW 21:22

Of him that taketh away thy goods ask them not again.

—LUKE 6:30

Ask bread.

—LUKE 11:11

Ask an egg.

—LUKE 11:12

Give the Holy Spirit to them that ask Him [equated to "good gifts"].*

—LUKE 11:13

To whom men have committed much, of him they will ask the more.

—LUKE 12:48

Ask drink.

—JOHN 4:9

Thou wouldest have asked of him, and he would have given thee living water.*

—JOHN 4:10

Whatever thou wouldst ask of God.

—JOHN 11:22

And whatever you shall ask in my name.

—JOHN 14:13

If ye ask anything in my name...

—JOHN 14:14

Ye shall ask what ye will.

—JOHN 15:7

Whatever ye shall ask...

—JOHN 15:16; 16:23

Hitherto have ye asked nothing in my name; ask, and ye shall receive, that your joy may be full.

—JOHN 6:24

Ask alms.

—ACTS 3:2

Above all that we ask or think.

—EPHESIANS 3:20

If any of you lack wisdom, let him ask of God... Let him ask in faith.*

—JAMES 1:5–6

Ye have not because ye ask not.

—JAMES 4:2

Ye ask, and receive not, because ye ask amiss"

—JAMES 4:3

Give an answer to every man that asks you a reason of the hope that is in you.*

—1 PETER 3:15

Whatever we ask.

—1 JOHN 3:22

If we ask anything...

—1 JOHN 5:14

Whatever we ask...

—1 JOHN 5:15

Notice that, except for the asterisk (*) items, the object of asking is generally indefinite and always, or at least primarily, material! The exceptions are one mention each of the Holy Spirit (Luke 11:13), living water (John 4:10), wisdom (James 1:5), and a "reason of the hope" (1 Peter 3:15).

There is a progression both within and between the respective heavenly realms. When we first move into the Christian experience by accepting the free gift of justification by faith, it does seem that we are hung up on receiving things, doesn't it? In fact, many so-called mature Christians, even spiritual Christians, seem to spend a lot of time in the first heaven, concerned with "more." But it is interesting that in this first realm we may also *ask* for the Holy Spirit and we may ask for "wisdom." Wisdom, you know, is different than knowledge. Knowledge is knowing the Word (the laver experience); wisdom is spiritual understanding of what the Word says, and, incidentally, this comes by the Holy Spirit.

Most of our time in the outer court, or first heaven, we spend asking for things. But when we begin to ask for the Holy Spirit, and are willing to be led by the Holy Spirit, rather than by the natural light, or logic, of men; and when we begin to ask for wisdom to understand the Word, the answer to the asking is really a recognition that we are ready to enter into the realm of the second heaven, where there is no natural light, but only the light of the lampstand, or Holy Spirit. We begin to mature and to progress.

In summary, the first level, the initiation of spiritual experience in Christ, sees Him coming. There is preoccupation with salvation (first coming) and second coming. There is identification, for example, through water baptism. This is the realm of beginnings and, consequently, immaturity; i.e., of asking. Most of the asking is for things.

You will recall that in the outer court is the altar, the place of salvation or justification, and the laver, the knowledge of the Word. Salvation and knowledge of the Word—this is where most Christians are. Now there are two perspectives we might want to keep in mind, especially as we consider this lowest realm of the heavenlies; that is, the person(s) being helped, and the person(s) helping or doing the ministering. You will recall that what the Levites did in the outer court was to help people get their sacrifices ready and to lay them on the altar. It was also the place where they met with the people and where they spoke the word to the people. This is a necessary, but lower level ministry. (See Ezekiel 44:10–14.) The people in the outer court are the unbelievers just coming in, new believers who are learning the Word, and the older believers who haven't matured because they haven't understood the Word they've heard, and therefore haven't entered into the holy place. The ministry or worker function is to lead others to Jesus, into salvation, and to teach the Word. Such is the first heaven.

But we can go beyond. We can begin to ask for the Holy Spirit and for wisdom to understand our knowledge of the Word. We can begin to move from passive grace ("ask, and it shall be given unto you") to active seeking ("Seek, and ye shall find").

What is the second heaven? The second heaven corresponds to the holy place. The holy place contains the lampstand which illustrates the light and power available from the Holy Spirit. Similarly, it contains the table of shewbread, which represents or reflects our ministry to one another, or what we call "body ministry." (Not one person ministering to a group, but each of us ministering to one another. That's the order in God.) The third element is the golden altar of incense, where we have praise and worship, prayer back to God. When we first enter in there is the lampstand—light and power *from* God. Then there is a stirring and a ministering *to one another*. And then there is a lifting it back *to* God in praise, worship, and prayer.

Scholars who look at the natural say that this second realm of the heavenlies is the "stars." Now, the stars are basically invisible, except that you can see an effect. You can see their light. The stars are millions of light-years away. The stars are bigger than our sun. The stars have more power and light than we can comprehend with our mind—but all that we can see is a little pinhead of light. The "stars" in Scripture represent two things: the "saints," the called out, born again believers; and, the "church," the local church. Let's look at the relevant scriptures.

Believers/Saints/Called-out Ones

> We have also a more sure word of prophecy, unto which ye do well that ye take heed, as unto a light that shineth in a dark place, until the day dawn, and the day star arise in your hearts.
>
> —2 PETER 1:19

The star is a symbol of the Spirit's illumination of the heart of one who follows Christ.

> Look toward heaven, and count the stars...So shall thy seed be.
>
> —GENESIS 15:5–6

See also Genesis 22:17; 26:4; Exodus 32:13; 2 Chronicles 27:23; Nehemiah 9:23; and Hebrews 11:12.

> The LORD your God hath multiplied you and, behold, ye are this day as the stars of heaven for multitude.
>
> —DEUTERONOMY 1:10; 10:22; 28:62

> I will exalt my throne above the stars of God.
>
> —ISAIAH 14:13

> Thou hast multiplied thy merchants above the stars of heaven.
>
> —NAHUM 3:16

The latter two references illustrate the attitude of Satan and Babylon toward the true saints of God.

Local church

> And He had in his right hand seven stars... The mystery of the seven stars which thou sawest in my right hand... The seven stars are the messengers of the seven churches.
>
> —REVELATION 1:16, 20;
> COMPARE TO REVELATION 2:1; 3:1

The second realm of the heavenlies, as seen by the representation of stars, is the place where believers function in the light of the Holy Spirit.

Let us recall that in the "request" trilogy, the first is "ask, and it shall be given to you"—it has to do with things primarily. The word "seek" is very interesting, because there is clearly a different order of objects associated with "seeking." There is a double reference to what seeking is, and is not, which provides a clear transition from the first to the second heavenly realm:

> Seek not what ye shall eat or what ye shall drink, neither be ye of doubtful mind. For all these things do the nations of the world seek after... But rather seek ye the Kingdom of God.
>
> —LUKE 12:29–31; COMPARE TO MATTHEW 6:31–33

This clearly puts us on notice that it is not things anymore. Then it says to *seek the Kingdom of God*. Let's look more specifically at what we should seek. The greatest number of references is clearly made to "seeking Jesus," beginning with Matthew 2:13 where it is recorded that "Herod will seek the young child to destroy Him." Others include Matthew 28:5; Mark 1:37; 3:32; 16:6; Luke 2:45; 2:48; 4:42; John 6:24; 6:26; 7:11; 7:34; 8:21; 11:56; 13:33; 18:8; 20:15.

As will be seen from the following references, there is clearly a deeper dimension to seeking than to asking.[1]

> Seeking rest.
>
> —Matthew 12:43

> Seeking goodly pearls.
>
> —Matthew 13:45

> Seeks that which is gone astray.
>
> —Matthew 18:12

> Seeking of Him a sign from heaven.
>
> —Mark 8:11

> Sought means to bring him in [for healing].
>
> —Luke 5:18

> The whole multitude sought to touch him.
>
> —Luke 6:9

> Sought of him a sign.
>
> —Luke 11:16

> Seeking rest.
>
> —Luke 11:24

> Sought fruit.
>
> —Luke 13:6

---

[1] There are also negative references. Rather than seek Him, the religious world's intention was to put Him to death. Examples in addition to Matthew 2:13: "sought to lay hands on Him"; "sought opportunity to betray Him"; and "sought false witness against Him" (Matt. 21:46; 26:59; 28:5).

Seeking fruit.

—Luke 13:7

Will seek to enter in at the narrow gate.

—Luke 13:24

Seek diligently till she find it [lost silver].

—Luke 15:8

Seek to save his life.

—Luke 17:33

Sought to see Jesus.

—Luke 19:3

To seek and to save the lost.

—Luke 19:10

The Father seeks such to worship Him.

—John 4:23

Seek not mine own will.

—John 5:30

Seek not honor.

—John 5:44

Seeks His glory that sent Him.

—John 7:18

Seek not mine own glory.

—John 8:50

Seek the Lord.

—Acts 17:27

Seek for glory and honor and immortality.

—Romans 2:7

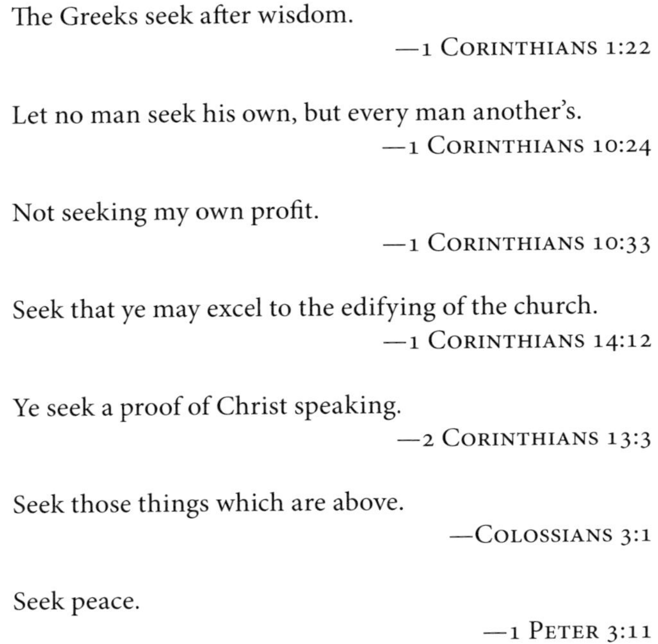

The Greeks seek after wisdom.

—1 CORINTHIANS 1:22

Let no man seek his own, but every man another's.

—1 CORINTHIANS 10:24

Not seeking my own profit.

—1 CORINTHIANS 10:33

Seek that ye may excel to the edifying of the church.

—1 CORINTHIANS 14:12

Ye seek a proof of Christ speaking.

—2 CORINTHIANS 13:3

Seek those things which are above.

—COLOSSIANS 3:1

Seek peace.

—1 PETER 3:11

Thus, in the second heaven it is not things anymore. We see that there is a seeking more of Jesus, the Kingdom, signs, the lost, where Jesus lives. The "nots" are just as important. At the front of the book we are told *not to seek things,* and toward the back we are warned against *seeking our own will or honor.*

In this middle realm we are dealing with the soul. It is spoken of as "being transformed by the renewing of your mind." The mind as it is renewed by the Holy Spirit, and in Christ, is no longer concerned with the things of this world, for self and those we love, but begins more and more to be concerned with the things of God, with that which is spiritual and above.

The lesson of John 1 is that in this realm we "follow" Jesus. Clearly the progression through the second heaven is, for most of us, a linear experience both in space and time. As we enter in there is a gradual unfolding of revelation and truth that draws us closer and closer to identification with the experience of Jesus. It has been pointed out that, in Philippians, there are three "fellowships" spoken of. The "fellowship of the gospel" (Phil. 1:5) is clearly an outer court, or first heaven, fellowship experience. The common denominator of this fellowship is Jesus as Savior. The "fellowship of the Spirit" (Phil. 2:1) relates to the second heaven, whereas "fellowship of His suffering" (Phil. 3:10) is most probably the golden altar experience which can be both second heaven and third heaven and is clearly the key to entrance within the innermost veil. This is also logical, because this innermost veil is the flesh (Heb. 10:20), and it is the flesh which suffers.

We are concerned here with the second heaven, the realm of the Spirit, and should see the concept of progression involved in the key words "followed Jesus" from John 1:37. We also saw earlier that "seek, and ye shall find" is the only one of the three "request" expressions in the active voice.

Personal experience generally parallels the historical sequence of revelation involved in the restoration of the tabernacle of David (Acts 15:16). Considering only that portion of the restoration having to do with this second realm, you will recall that the first distinctive worldwide outpouring of the Holy Spirit subsequent to the Reformation was in the early 1900s. This was a most definite "lampstand" experience relating to manifestation of the Spirit in power; i.e., various miracles and speaking in tongues. Classic Pentecostals who trace their origins to this period have, for the most part, not progressed beyond the adoration of past glories.

In 1948 there was a move of God, less well known, but with equal or greater impact in the spiritual realm. Sometimes called "Latter Rain," this move of the Spirit began in Saskatchewan, Canada. This move likewise was characterized by miracles, but also by the restoration of prophecy and the laying on of hands. Consequently, there was greater consciousness of the church as a body of believers. Movement from the lampstand to the table of shewbread, the Place of Communion, had begun.

The Charismatic Renewal that swept the world in the 1960s and early 1970s was clearly the "Table" experience. Brotherly love flowed. Doctrinal and denominational walls melted. The horizontal love flow, at the phileo level, was, and in some respects still is, intense. There was great consciousness of the body, the need for body ministry, and the establishment of church government according to the New Testament pattern.

Such movement is evident in the lives of individuals totally apart from historical moves. To give us a better feel for the progressive nature of this movement in the Spirit, another parenthesis may be in order. There are some who see in the Gospel of John, chapters 10–17, a clear picture of the tabernacle pattern expressed in Jesus teaching. There certainly seems to be some basis for drawing this parallel, particularly in light of the progressive nature of the Christian walk where each phase blends into the next. For reference, all of the parallels are shown here:

Door to the tabernacle—John 10

Brazen altar—John 11–12

Laver—John 13

Lampstand—John 14

Table of shewbread—John 15

Golden altar—John 16

Throne room (ark)—John 17

In the context of our discussion, let us begin with John 14. Note that John 14:1–6 serves as an introduction to the holy place, both by emphasizing that there are abodes, or places, prepared; and also in Jesus assertion that He is the "way" (lampstand), the "truth" (bread), and the "life." As regards the lampstand, specifically, note that John 14:12 asserts that we *shall* do *greater works!* The thrust of the remaining verses is that His place in the earth shall be taken by the Spirit—the manifestation of light and presence symbolized in the lampstand. The entrance into this second heavenly realm is always characterized by experience of, and awe at, the reality of the Holy Spirit as a real presence in life. (Hence, if we are not careful, we would begin to worship the Holy Spirit.) Note that the fourteenth chapter concludes with, "Arise, let us go from here."

The fifteenth chapter is where we go to—the bearing of fruit. Who benefits from the fruit? (Fruit, of course, is love, joy, peace, longsuffering, gentleness, goodness, faith, meekness, self control.) Others benefit! The source is "to abide in Christ"—this takes us back to the lampstand—but the function is for others. We are no longer servants but friends, because we have the mind of Christ (John 15:15). In comparing John 6:33 we see that to be bread is to give life to the world because we have lived by Him (John 6:33, 57). Hence, the restoration of body ministry, historically. For us personally, when we progress to this place we receive a revelation or awareness, that we are part of one body and that our function in Him is to minister to one another.

But there is a deeper identification in the communion of the Table—an identification with Jesus that places us squarely at odds with the world. This is a real paradox. Even as we know and live more of the love message of Christ, we shall begin to experience the resentment and persecution of those who are less spiritual, who are largely or totally governed by the values of this world. Already, even before chapter 16, there is a beginning of the fellowship of His suffering. Interestingly, chapter 15 concludes with a very significant, "Ye shall also bear witness." When compared with Revelation 6:9, this clearly points the way to the next experience which is at the golden altar/chapter 16.

> I saw under the altar the souls of them that were slain for the Word of God, and for the testimony which they held.
> —REVELATION 6:9

The message is clearer in chapter 16, which ends (v. 33) with the promise to us of tribulation in the world. But there is a tremendous promise in this chapter, veiled in mystery, but clearly identifiable with the golden altar of incense experience. That is, the product of travail shall be the birth of a manchild (v. 21), and there shall be great joy (v. 22), because then God shall speak plainly, no longer in proverbs or parables, or the "enigma" ("through a glass darkly") of 1 Corinthians 13:12 (vv. 25 and 29).

It seems that as we progress to this point, like the high priest on the Day of Atonement, or whenever the designated priest ministered alone at the golden altar, we are in some sense *alone* (compare to John 16:32). In fact, historically in the Scriptures, whenever man has been *face to face* with God, he has been alone.

This ministry to God at the golden altar is clearly a higher order ministry. On one occasion God was quite clear about the character of those who should minister in this place—Ezekiel 44:15–17.

> But the priests, the Levites, the sons of Zadok, who kept the charge of my sanctuary when the children of Israel went astray from me, they shall come near to me to minister unto me, and they shall stand before me to offer unto me the fat and the blood, saith the Lord God. They shall enter into my sanctuary, and they shall come near to my table, to minister unto me, and they shall keep my charge, and it shall come to pass that, when they enter in at the gates of the inner court, that they shall be clothed with linen garments; and *no wool shall come upon them,* while they minister in the gates of the inner court, and within... *They shall not gird themselves with anything*

> *that causeth sweat*... And they shall teach my people the difference between the holy and common, and cause them to discern between the unclean and the clean.
>
> —EZEKIEL 44:15–17, 23, EMPHASIS ADDED

Note especially the absence of wool—the garments of sweat and the curse. No element of man's own effort, no matter under what name or how sincerely the sweat effort was given, will be accepted by God. His desire is for worship and intercession on behalf of the saints (the set apart ones), which are the special functions associated with the golden altar and require vision of the nature of Christ, the Son of Man. This comes to those who are without guile (more on this later).

The paradox of the second heaven is that it is by the will of man ("seek, and ye shall find") that he progresses in spiritual revelation and understanding of the mind of God, yet the more he sees of God, the less he thinks of self. The real meaning of Philippians 2:5-8 becomes his own experience as he—

> ...knows Him, and the power of His resurrection, and the *fellowship of His sufferings,* being made conformable unto His death... Not as though I had already attained... But I *follow* after... Forgetting those things which are behind, and *reaching forth* unto those things which are before, *I press toward* the mark for the prize of the high calling of God in Christ Jesus.
>
> —PHILIPPIANS 3:10–14, EMPHASIS ADDED

The culmination of these thoughts by Paul is a reiteration that our citizenship is in heaven and that our body shall be changed (Phil. 3:20–21)!

It is noteworthy that in John 1:38, pursuant to "they followed Jesus," which is representative of the second heaven, the question is asked:

"Where do you abide?"

This, of course, brings us to the realm of the third heaven.

With regard to the third heaven, even the "naturalists" agree that this is where God dwells or abides. We find that in the tabernacle within the holy of holies is where God's presence was—where His glory rested! The Ark of the Covenant was His throne. And, we shall see that, for us, this is where we see Him in reality as Lord of All!

In terms of the tabernacle pattern, we see that the Lord dwelt between the Cherubim upon the Ark of the Covenant.

> And there will I meet with thee, and I will commune with thee from above the mercy seat, from between the two cherubim which are upon the ark of the testimony.
>
> —Exodus 25:22

> ...and Hezekiah prayed...O Lord God of Israel, who dwells between the cherubim, thou art the God, thou alone, of all the Kingdoms of the earth; thou hast made heaven and earth.
>
> —2 Kings 19:15

(Compare also to: 1 Samuel 4:4; 2 Samuel 6:2; 1 Chronicles 13:6; Psalm 80:1; Isaiah 37:16.)

Jesus Himself prayed to "Our Father, Who are in heaven." (Matt. 6:9). But many are the references to heaven as His dwelling place, and as the site of His throne.

Hear thou in heaven thy dwelling place.

—1 Kings 8:30

But our God is in the heavens.

—Psalm 115:3

O Thou who dwellest in the heavens.

—Psalm 123:1

For He hath looked down from the height of His sanctuary; from heaven did the Lord behold the earth.

—Psalm 102:19

The Lord hath prepared His throne in the heavens, and his Kingdom ruleth over all.

—Psalm 103:19

The Lord is in His holy temple, the Lord's throne is in heaven.

—Psalm 11:4

Thus saith the Lord: The heaven is my throne.

—Isaiah 66:1

We have such an high priest, who is seated on the right hand of the throne of the Majesty in the heavens, a minister of the sanctuary, and of the true tabernacle.

—Hebrews 8:1

Behold, a throne was set in heaven.

I heard a great voice of many people in heaven...Fell down and worshipped God that sat on the throne.

—Revelation 19:1–4

Perhaps the most explicit identification of the site of the throne as the third heaven (the sanctuary, or holy of holies) is found in Exodus 15:17, which, incidentally, represents the first usage of the applicable Hebrew word, and Jeremiah 17:12:

> Thou shalt bring them in, and plant them in the mountain of thine inheritance, in the place, O LORD which thou hast made for thee to dwell in, in the sanctuary, O LORD, which thy hands have established. The LORD shall reign forever and ever.
>
> —EXODUS 15:17–18

> A glorious high throne from the beginning is the place of our sanctuary.
>
> —JEREMIAH 17:12

Parenthetically, let us not forget that this throne is no ordinary throne, but is specifically identified with the righteousness, or holiness, of the Lord—

> God sits upon the throne of His holiness.
>
> —PSALM 47:8

Also, note in Psalm 48:1 that there is a "mountain of his holiness"—this is Mount Zion. (We shall refer to Zion again later.)

"Ask... Seek... Knock." There are the fewest number of scriptures associated with "knock"; in fact, only nine. Let us review them.

1. "Knock, and it shall be opened unto you" (Matt. 7:7).
2. "To him that knocks, it shall be opened" (Matt. 7:8).
3. "Knock, and it shall be opened unto you" (Luke 11:9).
4. "To him that knocks it shall be opened" (Luke 11:10).
5. "Let your loins be girded about, and your lamps burning; and ye yourselves like men that wait for their lord,

when he will return from the wedding; that when he cometh and knocketh, they may open unto him immediately… Be ye, therefore, ready also; for the Son of Man cometh at an hour when ye think not" (Luke 12:35–36, 40).

6. "Strive to enter in at the narrow gate; for many, I say unto you, will seek to enter in, and shall not be able. When once the Master of the house has risen up and shut the door, and ye begin to stand outside, and to knock at the door saying, Lord, Lord, open unto us; and he shall answer and say unto you, I know you not from where you are" (Luke 13:24–25).

   (Note the perfect correspondence of this message with the significance of the numeral "6," the number of "man." By way of contrast, the previous passage displays "grace," which is the significance of "5.")

7. "As Peter knocked at the door of the gate, a maid came to hearken, named Rhoda" (Acts 12:13).

8. "Peter continued knocking… [he] declared unto them how the Lord had brought him out of prison" (Acts 12:16).

9. "Behold, I stand at the door and knock; if any man hear my voice, and open the door, I will come into him… To him that overcometh will I grant to sit with me in my throne, even as I also overcame and am set down with my Father in His throne" (Rev. 3:20–21).

This last reference, standing in the numerical position of finality, judgment, and fruitfulness, is not, I believe, to be divorced from the passage immediately following where a "door was opened in heaven." What John saw there through the opened door was "a throne set in heaven" (Rev. 4:1–2).

You will recall that we equated the place of the throne with Mount Zion. This is another extremely significant theme in Scripture that we can't deal with here, except to affirm that Zion is where at least some of God's people are (or are going to be):

> Sing praise to the LORD who dwells in Zion.
>
> —PSALM 9:11

> The LORD dwells in Zion.
>
> —JOEL 3:21

> Oh my people that dwell in Zion.
>
> —ISAIAH 10:24

> Cry out and shout, thou inhabitant of Zion; for great is the Holy One of Israel *in the midst* of thee.
>
> —ISAIAH 12:6, EMPHASIS ADDED

> The LORD is exalted; for he dwells on high [in the heavenlies]; He hath filled Zion with justice and righteousness.
>
> —ISAIAH 33:5

> Therefore, the redeemed of the LORD shall return, and come with singing unto Zion, and everlasting joy shall be upon their head... And I have put my words in thy mouth, and I have covered thee in the shadow of Mine hand, that I may plant the heavens, and lay the foundation of the earth, and say unto Zion, thou art My people.
>
> —ISAIAH 51:11, 16

> Ye, also, as living stones, are built up a spiritual house...Wherefore also it is contained in the Scripture, behold, I lay in Zion a chief cornerstone...
>
> —1 PETER 2:5–6

There is a vision here which the Lord calls each of us to see. But, the words we have placed on this paper are not enough.

Each must pray for spiritual discernment, search the scriptures, and above all submit to the self-judgment of the priest at the golden altar that we may be without guile. This vision is simultaneously to see the Son of Man as the House of God wherein are the saints, and to see the purpose of God for the saints. And, finally, this vision and the experience of the purpose is not intellectually received nor is it unveiled to every Christian. If, in the next few pages, we can whet your appetite in this regard to "seek" and then to "knock," we shall rejoice together, in Him.

Going back to John 1, the day that corresponds to the experience of the third heaven is reflected in verses 43–51. Note especially the following (emphasis added):

> Jesus saw Nathaniel [Greek: "given of God"] coming to Him and saith of him, "Behold, an *Israelite* indeed, in whom is *no guile*."

Let us dwell on this a bit, for herein we see the circumstances and condition associated with "seeing." Clearly, in Nathaniel's name ("given of God") there is a confirmation that, as in the first heaven, there is grace involved. Recall that "knock, and it shall be opened" is likewise indicative that, once we have knocked, the actual revelation or unveiling, is passively received by the grace of the one who opens! The term "Israelite" signals to us that he was a member of the religious system—but, praise God, one who was not tainted thereby, for he had "no guile."

Guile (Greek: *dolos*) is "bait, snare, deceit." Let us look at each of the twelve usages of "dolos" in the New Testament.

1. "Then assembled together the chief priests, and the scribes, and the elders of the people, unto the palace of the high priest, who was called Caiphas, and consulted that they might take Jesus by subtlety [guile/dolos], and kill him. But, they said, Not on the Feast Day" (Matt. 26:3–5).

Guile here is clearly associated with the religious system, not only in the persons of the plotters themselves, but in their intent to observe a religious scruple even as they plotted murder.

2. "That which comes out of the man, that defiles the man. For from within, out of the heart of men, proceed evil thoughts... Deceit [guile/dolos]" (Mark 7:20–23).

   Guile comes from within and is associated with the heart, which, according to Jeremiah 17:9, is "deceitful above all things"—but it has an external expression.

3. The chief priests and the scribes sought how they might take him by craft [guile/dolos], and put him to death. But they said, Not on the Feast Day..." (Mark 14:1–2).

4. "Behold, an Israelite indeed in whom is no guile" (John 1:47).

5. "O, full of all subtlety [deceit/guile/dolos] and all mischief thou child of the Devil, enemy of all righteousness, wilt thou not cease to pervert the right ways of the Lord" (Acts 13:10).

   Guile here is again associated with perverting that which is of the Lord. Bar-Jesus was a false prophet, but he pretended to be of God. To be without guile is not to distort that which is of God, but to reflect Him clearly and accurately. Since God is love, and God is light (or holiness), love and holiness will characterize the ways of the man who is to see the Son of Man.

6. "Even as they did not like to retain God in their knowledge, God gave them over to a reprobate mind... Being filled with all unrighteousness... Deceit [guile/dolos]" (Rom. 1:28–29). The frame of reference here is similar to Acts 13:10.

7. "The more abundantly I love you, the less I be loved. But be it so, I did not burden you; nevertheless, being crafty [apparently an accusation made against him by some Corinthian Christians—a different word than dolos], I caught you with guile [dolos]" (2 Cor. 12:15–16).

8. "Our exhortation was not of deceit, nor of uncleanness, nor in guile (dolos); but as we were allowed of God to be put in trust with the gospel, even so we speak; not as pleasing men but God… Neither at any time used we flattering words…" (1 Thess. 2:3–5).

   This, and the remaining references, associate "guile" with speech. In this case, it is clear that to please men by flattering words (which is a common manifestation of all religious systems) is to deny the truth, and thereby to deceive. Such is not the man who will be privileged to see the fullness of the Son of Man.

9. "Wherefore, laying aside all malice, and all guile [dolos], and hypocrises, and envies, and all evil speakings, as newborn babies, desire the pure [sincere/unadulterated/without guile/adolos] milk of the Word…" (1 Pet. 2:1).

   The context here is 1 Peter 1:15, a call to be holy, which will manifest itself (that is, holiness will manifest itself) in our loving one another "with a pure heart" fervently: (v. 22). The Word of the Lord which endures forever is the word to be spoken. It is clear that "speaking" is associated with the manifested attitude of the heart and is that by which we shall be judged. A heart without guile is pleasing to the Lord. There is a play on words here as this represents the only New Testament usage of the Greek "adolos" meaning "without guile," or, more specifically, "pure and unadulterated." "Adolos" is used in secular writings of seed, corn, wheat, oil, wine, etc. Hence, again we are warned against the proclivity of "religious" teachers to mix the truth with untruth to serve their own ends. This can occur almost unconsciously, and is the reason that the Word indicates that it is the heart, rather than the mind, which must be dealt with.

10. "For even hereunto were ye called, because Christ also suffered for us, leaving us an example, that ye should follow in his steps; who did no sin, neither was guile [dolos] found in his mouth... But committed himself to Him that judges righteously" (1 Pet. 2:21–23).

    "In the same manner..." (1 Pet. 3:1).

    "In like manner... That your prayers be not hindered..." (1 Pet. 3:7).

11. "For he that will love life, and see good days, let him refrain his tongue from evil, and his lips that they speak no guile [dolos]; let him eschew evil, and do good; let him seek peace, and pursue it" (1 Pet. 3:10).

    To be without guile involves suffering and self sacrifice and, again, points to the tongue as the means of expression. Note that peace is the pursuit of one who walks in Jesus' steps. Also, recognizing that at the golden altar, whether outside or inside the veil, our function is intercession that the saints may be brought to perfection; to be without guile is essential if our prayers are to be effective.

12. "And I looked and, lo, a Lamb stood on Mount Zion, and with him an *144,000s,* having his Father's name written in their foreheads. And I heard a voice from heaven... And they sang as it were a new song before the throne... And no man could learn that song but the *144,000s,* who were redeemed from the earth. These are they who were not defiled with women; for they are virgins. These are they who *follow the Lamb* wherever He goes. These were redeemed from among men, the first fruits unto God and to the Lamb. And in their mouth

> was found *no guile*; for they are without fault before the throne of God" (Rev. 14:1–5, emphasis added).
>
> This reference, the twelfth, is the "governmental" reference, which is confirmed by identification with the 144 (12 x 12) thousands standing on Mount Zion (third heaven, dwelling place of God, and site of His throne) with the Lamb. Note that it is the Father's name ("Jah") that is written, and that there is a voice singing a new song before the throne. Those who could sing had been redeemed from the earth. It is their mouth that is without guile (dolos).

Taken together, these twelve references are exciting and give real insight as to why the man without guile shall "see." These are confirmed also in the Old Testament where there are three different Hebrew words that may be, and are, translated "guile." Three of those references are given here.

> If a man come presumptuously upon his neighbor, to slay him with guile...
>
> —Exodus 21:14

Could guile equal presumption? Certainly there is presumption wherever deceit or pride cause us to break peace.

> Blessed is the man... In whose spirit there is no guile.
>
> —Psalm 32:1–2

Compare with 1 Chronicles 22:6–9, wherein we see David forbidden to build the House of God because he had shed blood. Rather, this was to be left to Solomon, "a man of rest." "I will give peace and quietness unto Israel in his days."

> Keep thy...Lips from speaking guile. Depart from evil and do good; seek peace, and pursue it.
>
> —Psalm 34:13–14

Going back to John 1, the promise is made that the man in whom is no guile...

> ...shall see greater things than these.
>
> —JOHN 1:50

Nathaniel was seen by Jesus even before Philip called him, and presumably was out of eyesight! Yet the sight, or vision, of Nathaniel should be more penetrating.

> And He saith unto him, verily, verily, I say unto you, hereafter ye shall see heaven open, and the angels [messengers] of God ascending and descending upon the Son of Man.
>
> —JOHN 1.51

This promise ties directly to Jacob's dream of a ladder extending from earth to heaven (Gen. 28:12). The message of Jehovah the Lord to Jacob in the dream was:

> And, behold, I am with thee, and will keep thee in all places to which thou goest, and will bring thee again into this land.
>
> —GENESIS 28:25

> And Jacob awaked out of his sleep, and he said, surely the LORD is in this place; and I knew it not. And he was afraid, and said, how awesome [dreadful] is this place! This is none other but the house of God, and this is the gate of heaven.
>
> —GENESIS 28:16–17

By comparing John 1:51 with Genesis 28:17 we see confirmation that the House of God is the Son of Man. Who is the Son of Man? He is Christ, of whom Jesus, the Son of God, is Head. For example, Paul's prayer for us in Ephesians 1:17–23 is that we might receive:

> The spirit of wisdom and revelation of Him, the eyes of your understanding being enlightened [to see that He is] ... the head over all to the church, which is His body, the fullness of Him that filleth all in all.

While Jesus was on earth He was also Christ—there was only the Head—but the Head now has an ever growing body which by travail of the saints shall give birth to the company who shall stand in Zion with the Lamb.

Perhaps I have strayed too far and prolonged this discussion too long. Let us quickly recall that John 17, which Scofield calls "Christ's High Priestly, Intercessory Prayer," pictures for us the function of believers at the golden altar, even within the veil. The world has been overcome (John 16:33). Life eternal is seen not to be time related, but life is the increasing knowledge of the true God (John 17:3). This we would expect, for in this realm we are in His presence!

Can you and I become the "I" in John 17? This is the intention and purpose to which we are called (vv. 18, 22–24). It is for *now*, if we would enter in. Do not rationalize away Jesus' words as in some measure future-spective. We do ourselves a disservice if we doubt that Jesus meant what He said. He said:

> And now I am no more in the world...
>
> —John 17:11

> Father, I will that they also, whom thou has given me, be with me where I am, that they may behold My glory.
>
> —John 17:24

Seek, and ye shall find. Knock, and the door shall be opened. We do, however, enter alone, even as Jacob. There is a dying involved, even the death of the cross. May we each "turn our eyes upon Jesus, and look full in his wonderful face, that the things of earth may grow strangely dim in the light of His glory and grace."

3 – The Lie

I HAVE BEEN KNEELING here for some time now, with my Bible open, and some notes before me, but mostly with my heart full of the revelation of Jesus Christ. I know I have been holding back, reticent, because I'm not certain that it's possible to put on this piece of paper the breadth and depth of that which the Lord has allowed me to see.

I'm fearful, also, that except for a faithful few, this word will be found offensive and repulsive by many, resulting in rejection. Now, I know we are to rejoice in rejection, particularly when we are persecuted for righteousness' sake, and yet there is something in each of us, in our flesh, that shuns rejection, shies aways from it, seeks to avoid it.

The crux of the matter is that, while many are called (in fact, all are called, for "God so loved the (whole) world..."), there are many fewer who are chosen, and fewer still of the chosen who are faithful (Rev. 17:14).

One of the reasons that I'm having so much difficulty getting started is that much, or all, of what I have to share with you is the result of three or four years of waiting on the Lord, seeking to know the "truth." How can this be capsulated into a few pages? Now, I know that the truth sets us free, and I praise God for that, for surely as we see the truth and walk in the truth, though the whole world abandon us, yet we can rest in the knowledge that we have seen the vision of the reality of God in the midst of His people! In Romans 3:3, we read, "What does it matter if some do not believe? Shall their unbelief make the faithfulness of God without effect? God forbid. Let God be true (even though this make) every man a liar. As it is written, 'That you might be justified in your sayings, and might overcome when you are judged.'" In other words, if you are true, if you see the truth and are walking in the truth, then it matters not whether any other man has seen the truth. You can know—you will be judged as one who has overcome the world!

The World vs. the Church

The fundamental problem with Christians and the Christian church today is that we have been deceived into departing from the Truth. The Lie has so long been believed as truth that we don't recognize the truth as truth, but call it heresy and error. The big stumbling block in the life of almost every believer, and hence the rock of offense to our so-called "churches," is the world. Notwithstanding our doctrines, our theologies, the spiritual songs and hymns that we sing, we have not, in reality, abandoned the world. The world is beautiful and attractive; it promises great rewards to those who take her mark, to those who are called by her name. And, because we are attracted to the world's offerings, even as Balaam was to the riches of Balak the Moabite, we do everything in our power to justify ourselves; and we continue to walk in the way of the world.

Jesus was able to say, at the end of His walk on this earth, "I have overcome the world" (John 16:33). He hadn't yet gone to the cross—it has nothing to do with the cross—rather, He overcame the world in the sense that He refused to sin, he refused to become a part of the world system though He could have been its ruler. Rather, He *is,* in John 17, living in the heavenly realm. In John 17:24 He prays, "Father, I will that they also, whom you have given me, be with me where I am that they may behold my glory which you have given me."

Jesus was right here, with His feet on the earth, but He was not in the world. He was living even then in the heavenly realm. His prayer, His desire is that we, too, might live in this heavenly realm—for it is in the heavenlies that we see His glory. Recall that our blessings are in the heavenlies. No matter what teachings may be derived from Scripture indicating that we shall prosper in the earthly realm, recall that our blessings, according to Ephesians 1:3, are "in the heavenlies in Christ." Why? Because He has chosen us in Himself before the world began, that we should be holy and without blame before Him, in love, "having predestinated us unto the adoption of sons by Jesus Christ to Himself."

It is true, particularly in the Old Testament, that we read much about the believers having blessings in this world, but those blessings were essentially Old Covenant blessings. They were associated with Judaism. Judaism was a religion associated with the world. The religion of Judaism, while it was originally established and ordained by God, had its root in the "knowledge of good and evil" associated with the fall of man as he sought to exalt himself in the world (Gen. 3:5–6, with 1 John 2:15–17). God began a new order, a new creation, in Jesus Christ—a creation that takes its sustenance, not from the tree of the knowledge of good and evil, but from the tree of life. This life is from the Holy Spirit, springing up as a fountain within us, as rivers of living water. For, surely, it says in Romans 8:14 that "as many as are led by the Spirit of God, they are the Sons of God." Note that "Sons of God" are not those who know good and evil, but those who are led by the Spirit, by life in Christ Jesus. It is not yet made apparent who these Sons of God are (1 John 3:2), but this glory shall be revealed (1 John 3:2–3), and the Sons of God will be made manifest (Rom. 8:19).

Already, we have established in just these few paragraphs the counterpoint between Judaism and the church of Jesus Christ. We have established as counterpoint the religion, or way, of this world and divine life, with blessings in the heavenly realm.

What we find, you see, is that the church has adopted Judaism. This thrust began early, necessitating the Galatian letter and the first church Council at Jerusalem. It is still very much with us.

Let me pose a few questions for your consideration concerning the Book of Revelation. The Book of Revelation, I am coming to see more and more, is in fact a glimpse behind the scene of God's present day sovereign dominion and the working of His purposes in men as He prepares Himself an eternal dwelling place. All too often we read Revelation 1:3 and keep on going. But, instead let's pause and look at it for a moment (emphasis added):

> Blessed is He that reads, and they that hear the words of *this prophecy,* and keep [watch over, preserve] those things which are written in it, *for the time is at hand.*

Notwithstanding this admonition, there is a tendency to dismiss everything beyond chapter 3, or perhaps chapter 5, as not applying to Christians, and especially not to Christians who are alive today. But I submit to you that "this prophecy" is a very particular prophecy. Revelation itself seems to confirm this by defining "prophecy":

> For the testimony of Jesus is the spirit of prophecy.
>
> —Revelation 19:10

John fell at the feet of a man to worship him. But the man rebuked him, saying, "Worship me not. I am your fellow servant, and of your brethren, that have the testimony of Jesus. Worship God; for the testimony of Jesus is the spirit of prophecy."

Even as these words were spoken, John "saw heaven opened" (v. 11). He saw heaven opened, and, as he looked into it, he saw the Word of God (v. 13), the King of kings (v. 16). This book, this prophecy, is a testimony of Jesus! It is a vision of the church as seen from God's perspective—for the church is Jesus Christ on earth.

Turn to Revelation 13 where we see one standing upon the "sand of the sea." Could this sand be Abraham's earthly seed (Gen. 22:17; 32:12)? The sea, you will recall, symbolizes the chaotic mass of humanity, which is the world. Out of the midst of the sea comes a beast.

This beast has "seven heads and ten horns, and upon his horns ten crowns, and upon his heads the name of blasphemy." Back in Revelation 17:3 we see that the name is "names" of blasphemy—with "blasphemy" meaning literally "sayings which hinder." We know from Daniel that these seven heads and ten horns have to do with the world system. "Seven" signifies "spiritual perfection" and "ten" signifies "human responsibility." Hence, these "sayings which hinder" have the appearance of spiritual works. They do not represent hellish lies in the traditional sense, but rather masquerade as Christian truth, but with the effect of diverting attention from the truth, which is Jesus Christ manifest in the flesh, wherein is reflected the relationship between the Father and the Son. (See 1 John 4:3 and 2:22)

This beast was like:

- "A leopard"—spotted, symbolic of confusion (Jer. 13:23 with Jude 12); a stealthy observer (Hos. 13:7); special enemy of "cities" (Jer. 5:6), remembering that cities are the only legitimate local manifestation of the church of Jesus Christ.

- "Feet like a bear"—feet of the bear are indiscriminate (2 Sam. 17:8; Prov. 28:15); steals lambs (1 Sam. 17:34); lies in wait (Lam. 3:10); devours flesh (Dan. 7:5); tears fat of heart (Hos. 13:8).

- "Mouth of a lion"—steals lambs (1 Sam. 17:34); devours (1 Pet. 5:8); tears in pieces (Nah. 2:12); lies in wait secretly (Ps. 10:9).

The leopard is swift, the bear is ponderous, the lion is secretive. These, and the other attributes above, describe the various attributes which Satan exhibits in his opposition to the church of Jesus Christ. Regardless of the method, the objective is the same; that is, to steal lambs (young sheep who have not reached maturity)!

The beast receives "his power, and his throne and great authority" from the dragon, which is Satan (compare to Rev. 12:3). This dragon is Satan in his role as prince of the world (John 14:30).

> And I saw one of his heads as though it were wounded to death; and his deadly wound was healed, and all the world wondered after the beast. And they worshipped the dragon who gave power unto the beast; and they worshipped the beast, saying 'who is like the beast? Who is able to make war with him?
>
> —Revelation 13:3–4

The beast obviously represents Satan's dominion. It is the power of this world. Is Satan's power natural or spiritual? I believe it is undeniable that Satan's power is spiritual, although it can manifest itself in political (natural) power. Notice, for example, how most, if not all, kings, emperors, etc., have ascribed to themselves deity, and have longed to be worshipped.

What do the seven heads represent? Isaiah 9:14–16 indicates that "head" represents "ancient and honorable" leaders of the people. The "head" is one of the aspects or areas of dominion exercised by Satan through the world system—that is, through organized humanity. This is confirmed by Revelation 17:9.

Could this "head with the deadly wound that was healed" be Judaism? Was not Judaism dealt a deathblow on two occasions? The first time was the destruction of Jerusalem, and extinction of the kingly line associated with the Babylonian captivity of

Judah. Who breathed life back into Judaism? Was it not the King of Persia? Was he, in turn, not subject to the Prince of Persia, a satanic angel given authority by Satan (Dan. 10:13, 20)?

Was not Judaism given a second, and more decisive death blow on the cross at Calvary? Twice, Judaism was left for dead! Both times the world system healed its wound and restored its life. Could it be that this second revival of Judaism is the beast of Revelation 13:11-12? That is, the manifestation of Judaism within the church, which is called the "synagogue of Satan" in Revelation 2:9 and 3:9, "Satan's throne" in 2:13, and the "depths of Satan" in 2:24?

This beast, it is recorded, opened his mouth in blasphemy ("sayings that hinder") against God "to blaspheme His name, and His tabernacle ['dwelling place,' meaning 'God's people'], and them that dwell in heaven [the heavenlies]. And it was given unto him to make war with the saints, and to overcome them; and power was given him over kindreds, and tongues, and nations."

Is this not the church, the institutional, traditional confusion known as the church as it is dominated by the world system?

> And all that dwell upon the earth shall worship him, whose names are not written from the foundation of the world in the Book of life of the Lamb slain from the foundation of the world, "if any man have an ear, let him hear."
>
> —Revelation 13:8–9

In considering this matter, it might be well to ask whether there is a difference between the "Book of life" and the "Book of life of the Lamb."

<table>
<tr><th>Book of Life</th><th>Book of Life of the Lamb</th></tr>
<tr><td>Rev. 3:5—Overcomers not blotted from Book of Life</td><td>Rev. 13:8—Will NOT worship the Beast</td></tr>
<tr><td>Rev. 17:8—Those NOT in Book of Life shall wonder at the Beast</td><td rowspan="2">Rev. 21:27—Those in Lamb's book enter New Jerusalem ("Those who love and make a lie are outside" [Rev. 22:15])</td></tr>
<tr><td>Rev. 20:12—Dead were judged out of those things written in the books according to their works; one book was Book of Life</td></tr>
<tr><td colspan="2">Rev. 20:15—Whosoever NOT found in Book of Life cast into Lake of Fire (compare to Rev. 22:19); can lose share by detracting from words of this prophecy</td></tr>
<tr><td colspan="2">Phil. 4:3—Names of Paul's fellow workers are in the Book of Life (compare to Rev. 20:12); that indicates there is more than one book</td></tr>
</table>

> He that leads into captivity shall go into captivity; he that kills with the sword must be killed with the sword. Here is the patience and faith of the saints.
>
> —Revelation 13:10

The first portion of Rev. 13:10 seems to affirm that the captivity of Judah is in view. With respect to the "sword," the "sword" is symbolic of the Word of God in the Scriptures. The Beast is using the Word of God (2 Cor. 3:10 "the letter kills") to destroy the true saints.

Such was the practice of the Pharisees; it is likewise with many believers today. Ultimately, however, that same Word of God shall be used by the Spirit to slay the beast.

Read the rest of Revelation 13:11–18 and 14:1.

Could the two horns of the bloodless lamb be "faith and love," the two witnesses, without "hope"? Notice that the whole objective is to deceive by means of an "image," or likeness, of the beast. Just as the true church is to be made in the image and likeness of God as manifested in Christ Jesus, so does this image reflect that which is counterfeit.

Notice that there are three distinctives associated with worship of the beast: "the mark," "the name," and "the number of the name" (i.e., the number of a man—"666" = perfection of imperfection).

Compare this with the 144,000s of faithful chosen. They stand on Mount Zion and have the Father's name written on their forehead—"I AM"; or, Everpresent life. Those who have been deceived are contented with a man's name, such as Wesley, or Baptist, or Lutheran, or Charismatic, or Whatever. But, there is no other name, under heaven, given among men, whereby we must be saved except the name Jesus (Acts 4:12). Remember that "Jesus" means "Jehovah is Salvation."

The number associated with the faithful chosen is 12 x 12 x 10 x 10—human responsibility under divine government; 12 = 3 x 4, or God and His creation joined together in divine government. By contrast, "666" represents man as divinity, a government unto himself.

What is the "mark of the beast"? It is the "mark of his name" (Rev. 14:9–11) which is the system which governs how we think ("forehead") and what we do ("hand"). How sad that we have traded the simplicity of God's life in love for the complexity of man's traditions, dogmas, doctrines, and rules that dictate how God's people should worship and live. For example, does your local assembly or denomination have a constitution or discipline? Is there a formal dogma associated with "membership"?

The tragedy is that today most Christians are more quick to defend the human/earthly name that they bear (that is, the church name or denominational name, the doctrinal or creedal name) than the name of Jesus Christ. In fact, time after time you will find the name of Jesus put down that the name of man may be exalted. (For example, look at any church sign: Is Jesus' name at the top?)

I read two books recently that helped bring these thoughts into focus, and had a profound impact in confirming the vision that I am sharing here.

The first and longest is *The Orthodoxy of the Church* by Watchman Nee.[1] I encourage you to obtain and read this book. One of the most important points that Watchman Nee makes is that, with respect to the church today, we must deal explicitly with the seven letters to the seven representative local churches recorded in Revelation, chapters 2 and 3. These letters have to do with the reality of the church's condition before God, and prescribe the remedy. The call for "overcomers" is not for us to be special, or "superspiritual," but that we should be "normal" Christians. Abnormality has become normality, so that to be normal in God's sight will make us appear abnormal in the sight of the church people who are being deceived and dominated by the beast, the world system, and the exaltation of self.

In each of the seven churches, which together typify the church as it is today, you will find a line of opposition. In Ephesus and Pergamos there was Nicolaitanism ("conquerors of the people"), the concept of a separate ruling or governing eldership class that is better than, and separate from, the rest of the people. This approach excuses the people from needing to know God themselves, and keeps them from growing up and going on beyond the ABCs (Heb. 6:1).

In the letters to Smyrna and Philadelphia there is reference to those "who call themselves Jews, but are not." These are explicit references to the adoption of Judaistic doctrine and practice into the church. In other letters there is reference to Balaam (where money becomes the governing factor, and the church is run as a business) and to Jezebel (who causes the church to actually turn from God and to worship the idols of the world). In Sardis there is multiplicity of names, and deadness, while in Laodicea (the church of "people's opinions") there is spiritual pride.

Watchman Nee draws attention to four main points of difference between Judaism and the church as seen in the purposes of God:

1. The temple
2. The law
3. The priests
4. The promises

The Jews built a splendid temple of stone and gold as their place of worship. The ten commandments and a myriad of other regulations constituted a written code of conduct, or standard of behavior. To attend to spiritual affairs they had the office of the priests, a group of special people. Lastly, they had the promise of blessings by which they may prosper on this earth.

Contrast this with God's purpose for the church. There is no place of stone and gold, no temple, for we the people are the temple (Eph. 2:21–22). We have no need for laws, for the law of the Spirit of life is within us. Hebrews 8 and Jeremiah 31 tell us that right or wrong is not written on tablets of stone, or pages of paper, but in the heart. In the church, all are to be priests (1 Pet. 2:9). But like the Jews, we restrict the spiritual tasks of baptism and sacraments, and teaching, to a special class of people. Rather, everyone should be serving the Lord. To do "secular" things is but to take care of our daily needs. Finally, with respect to promises, what the Scriptures teach is not how much we gain before God, but how much we will be able to let go before God. The true church does not consider that suffering is a painful thing, but counts it all joy (James 1:2).

The second booklet is particularly poignant. This booklet is entitled *The Waning Authority of Christ in the Churches* by A.W. Tozer.[2] The author deplores the situation in the church, and acknowledges that he himself is very much involved in the situation he deplores. He wrote in 1963; since then the situation has not improved, but worsened. Let me provide a few quotations to whet your appetite. I strongly recommend that you obtain and read the whole booklet. Then cry in private!

> Among the gospel churches Christ is now in fact little more than a beloved symbol. "All Hail the Power of Jesus' name" is the church's national anthem and the cross is her official flag, but in the week-by-week services of the church and the day-by-day conduct of her members someone else, not Christ, makes the decisions. Under proper circumstances Christ is allowed to say "Come unto me, all ye that labor and are heavy laden" or "Let not your heart be troubled," but when the speech is finished someone else takes over. Those in actual authority decide the moral standards of the church, as well as all objectives and all methods employed to achieve them. Because of long and meticulous organization it is now possible for the youngest pastor just out of seminary to have more actual authority in a church than Jesus Christ has....
>
> What we do is this: We accept the Christianity of our group as being identical with that of Christ and His apostles. The beliefs, the practices, the ethics, the activities of our group are equated with the Christianity of the New Testament. Whatever the group thinks or says or does is scriptural, no questions asked. It is assumed that all our Lord expects of us is that we busy ourselves with the activities of the group. In so doing we are keeping the commandments of Christ....
>
> But I suppose I should offer some concrete proof to support my charge that Christ has little or no authority today among the churches. Well, let me put a few questions and let the answers be the evidence.
>
> What church board consults our Lord's words to decide matters under discussion?....Board meetings are habitually opened with a formal prayer or "a season of prayer"; after that the Head of the church is respectfully

> silent while the real rulers of the church take over. Let anyone who denies this bring forth evidence to refute it. I for one will be glad to hear it....
>
> The prayer before the meeting is for divine help to carry out their plans. Apparently the idea that the Lord might have some instructions for them never so much as enters their heads....
>
> What then are we to do? Each one of us must decide, and there are at least three possible choices. One is to rise up in shocked indignation and accuse me of irresponsible reporting. Another is to nod general agreement with what is written here but take comfort in the fact that there are exceptions, and we are among the exceptions. The other is to go down in meek humility and confess that we have grieved the Spirit and dishonored our Lord in failing to give Him the place His Father has given Him as Head and Lord of the church. Either the first or the second will but confirm the wrong. The third if carried out to its conclusion can remove the curse. The decision lies with us.

A decision lies with us; what is that decision? That decision, essentially, is to follow Jesus. As it says in Revelation 14:4:

> Those who are not defiled with women, those who are virgins, those who can sing the new song before the throne, these are they who follow the Lamb wherever He goes, these [will be] redeemed from among men, [as] the first fruits unto God and to the Lamb, and in their mouth is found no guile, for they are without fault before the throne of God.

This decision requires more than just singing the song, "I have decided to follow Jesus." It means wearing garments of righteousness. This is not the righteousness that we have in Christ before the Father, but are garments of righteous works (compare to Rev. 3:4, 16:15) that will enable us to stand unashamed before the person of our Lord Jesus Christ at His appearing.

The great mystery is how a "faithful city" could become a "harlot" (Isa 1:21). How could the beautiful woman in Revelation 12 also be described in Revelation 17 as the "woman sit[ting] upon a scarlet colored beast, full of names of blasphemy, having seven heads and ten horns... The woman drunk with the blood of the saints, and with the blood of the martyrs [witnesses] of Jesus"?

> I wondered with great wonder.

This condition of the church is deplorable. It has nothing to do with the salvation of those who believe not in Jesus Christ. Rather, it has to do with the disobedience of those who have believed and who have been born again. It has to do with those who will be overthrown in the wilderness because God is displeased with them. (See 1 Corinthians 10:5.) Why is God not pleased? Because we lust after evil things, we are idolaters, because we commit fornication, because we put Christ to the test, because we murmur and complain (1 Cor. 10:6–11).

> Wherefore, let him who thinks he stands, take heed lest he fall!
>
> —1 CORINTHIANS 10:12

This is really the problem of Laodicea. As you will see in Watchman Nee's book, referenced above, Laodicea is nothing more than fallen Philadelphia—Philadelphia fallen because of her pride in her spiritual knowledge and in her spiritual accomplishments, And as she became prideful, she lost the life, and ceased to walk in love.

I believe, in some measure, 1 and 2 Thessalonians correspond, respectively, to Philadelphia and Laodicea in terms of the impact of their messages. What has caused the church to fall? Why are believers in danger of perdition ("ruin")?

The Lie vs. the Truth

This brings us to the heart of the matter: THE LIE. Second Thessalonians 2:11 states quite matter of factly that believers (whose faith isn't growing and whose love isn't abounding and whose patience isn't enduring in persecutions and tribulations [2 Thess. 1:3–4]) will believe "The Lie." Notice, it isn't "believe *a* lie," it is "believe The Lie" (2 Thess. 2:11, NIV). What is this lie?

There is only "one" lie; hence, "The Lie." It is the original lie recorded in Genesis 3:3–6: you shall not die if you know good and evil. Rather, if you know good and evil, you shall be as God. Moreover, the knowledge of good and evil is presented as beneficial to the body ("good for food"), and to the soul ("pleasant to the eyes"), and to the spirit ("desired to make wise"); hence, the necessity for Paul to pray for these Thessalonian Christians, in 1 Thessalonians 5:23, that "your whole spirit and soul and body be preserved blameless unto the coming ("presence"—*parousia*) of our Lord Jesus Christ. Faithful is He that calls you, who will do it." We cannot preserve ourselves, and especially not by the knowledge of good and evil, but only as we depend on the Lord Jesus Christ for His life-giving Spirit.

While readers of these words will concur that these are Scripture, already most readers are rationalizing that the meaning dare not be taken literally. After all, isn't it the function of the church to teach the difference between good and evil? Not at all! The function of the church is to provide a habitation, or dwelling place, for the eternal God.

Compare Deuteronomy 1:39. Jehovah was angry with His people, Israel, because they rebelled against His commandment (v. 26) and did not believe His promise of life (v. 32). So Jehovah told them that they would not receive the promise of entering the land (v. 35). Rather, He told them that their babies and children who "had *no* knowledge between good and evil" shall go in and possess the inheritance (v. 39). Jesus was referring to this same requirement when He says, "Except ye be converted [turned about], and become as little children, you shall not enter into the Kingdom of heaven" (Matt. 18:3–4).

Lest someone cite Hebrews 5:14 as a contradiction, let me clarify the meaning of that passage which confirms, rather, that the discernment of good and evil comes not from knowledge, but from "spiritual senses." First Corinthians 2:13–14 emphasizes that "discernment" derives not from "words which man's wisdom teaches, but which the Holy Spirit teaches." The "things of the Spirit of God...are spiritually discerned." Philippians 1:9 associates this discernment ("judgment" in the King James Version) with abounding love.

In John, chapter 8, Jesus specifically identifies "the devil" as the one who speaks "The Lie" (v. 44). This is compared with "the truth" which makes us "free" (v. 32). Between these two passages relating to "the truth" and "The Lie," Jesus recognizes that the Jews are the natural seed of Abraham (the sand of the seashore), but indicates that they are not Abraham's spiritual seed (the stars of the sky) because they seek to kill Jesus, and because Jesus' word has no place in them (v. 37). By comparing all the associated scriptures, we can clearly see the difference between "the truth" and "The Lie."

The Truth	The Lie
Light of life (v. 12)	Walking in darkness (v. 12)
Judge no man (v. 15)	Judge after the flesh (v. 15)
From above (v. 23)	From beneath (v. 23)
Not of this world (v. 23)	Of this world (v. 23)
Do nothing of myself (v. 28)	Speaks on his own (v. 44)

Do always those things that please (God) the Father (v. 29)	Do lusts of your Father the Devil (v. 44)
Continue in my Word (v. 31)	My Word has no place in you (v. 37)
Love Jesus (v. 42)	Seek to kill Jesus (vv. 37, 40)
Acknowledge the Father (vv. 26, 28, 29)	No Father (v. 44)
Sent by God (v. 42)	Came of self (v. 42)
Hear God's words (v. 47)	Hear not God's words (v. 47)
Seeks not own glory (v. 50)	Seeks own glory (vv. 42, 44)
Never see death (vv. 51, 54)	Die in your sins (v. 21)
Know God (v. 55)	Know *not* God, *but think you do* (vv. 54–55)

The last comparison is the sorrow of the matter. It is a tragedy that is being repeated this very hour throughout the visible church in every local assembly. There is positive conviction and assurance that we know God, yet few hear *His* Words. There is, rather, the seeking of glory and honor for self in this world, judging after the flesh in the knowledge of right and wrong, and emphasis on "walking," which is "darkness," rather than on "living" ("life") which is "light." God is not calling us "to do," but "to be" witnesses (Acts 1:8)—"to be" is as simple as "to love Jesus and to love your neighbor as yourself."

> You need not that any man teach you; but as the same anointing ["unction from the Holy One"] teaches you of all things, and is truth, and is no lie... You shall abide in him"
>
> —1 John 2:27

The truth, then, is *not knowledge* of good and evil, *but to abide in Him* who is life.

If the truth is so simple and straightforward, why have we come to believe The Lie? What else is involved in The Lie? This leads us to a more detailed examination of 1 and 2 Thessalonians, especially 2 Thessalonians 2.

If the epistles of Paul to the churches and those of Jesus Christ through John to the churches are aligned, we see this comparison:

Romans	**To Ephesus**
Corinthians	**To Smyrna**
Galatians	**To Pergamum**
Ephesians	**To Thyatira**
Philippians	**To Sardis**
Colossians	**To Philadelphia**
Thessalonians	**To Laodicea**

While I am not here going to expound these relationships, there is a correspondence between Thessalonians and Laodicea wherein Laodicea represents a falling away.

This is very striking in the context of 1 and 2 Thessalonians taken together. First Thessalonians is unique among all of Paul's letters in that he ascribes to them (1:3) all three virtues of 1 Corinthians 13:13:

> "your work of faith"
> "labor of love"
> "patience of hope"

Now compare this with Paul's introduction to 2 Thessalonians. In 2 Thessalonians 1:3 they are commended because:

> "your faith grows exceedingly"
> "love toward each other abounds"

They are commended for "patience and faith" in persecution and tribulation, but explicit mention of "hope" is missing. In fact, 2 Thessalonians 2:2 gives evidence that they have lost their hope, even as faith and love grows and abounds.

In 1 Thessalonians wherein was faith, love, and hope, they are commended because:

> They had turned from idols (1 Thess. 1:9).
>
> > To serve the true and living God (1 Thess. 1:9).
> >
> > To wait for his Son from heaven (1 Thess. 1:10).
>
> They had received the Word of God, not as the word of men, but as truth (1 Thess. 2:13).

Paul's concern for them is essentially positive. He desires that they:

> Not be moved by afflictions (1 Thess. 3:3).
>
> Stand fast in the Lord (1 Thess. 3:8).
>
> Increase and abound even more in love (1 Thess. 3:12).
>
> That they may be unblameable in holiness at the coming (*parousia*) of the Lord with all His saints (1 Thess. 3:13).
>
> Increase more and more in love (1 Thess. 4:10).
>
> Do your own business (1 Thess. 4:11).
>
> Work with own hands (1 Thess. 4:11).

> Not be ignorant concerning the coming (*parousia*) of the Lord (1 Thess. 4:13–18).
>
> Not sleep, but watch and be sober-minded (1 Thess. 5:6).
>
> Put on breastplate of faith and love and, for an helmet, the hope of salvation (1 Thess. 5:8).
>
> Have their whole spirit, soul, and body preserved blameless unto the coming (*parousia*) of the Lord Jesus Christ (1 Thess. 5:23).

In 2 Thessalonians on the other hand, because hope has been shaken, we find a distinctively negative connotation. We find they:

> Are troubled (2 Thess. 1:7).
>
> May not be counted worthy of His calling (2 Thess. 1:11).
>
> May not fulfill all the good pleasure of His goodness (2 Thess. 1:11).
>
> May not fulfill the work of faith with power (2 Thess. 1:11).
>
> May not have the name of the Lord Jesus glorified in them (2 Thess. 1:12).
>
> May not be glorified in Him (2 Thess. 1:12).
>
> Are shaken in mind and troubled that they have missed His *parousia* (that is, they have lost their hope) (2 Thess. 2:2).

What is "hope"? In comparing Ephesians 6:17 (helmet of salvation) and 1 Thessalonians 5:8 (helmet, hope of salvation) we see that salvation and hope are equivalent. "Salvation" literally means "deliverance" or "preservation." This deliverance/preservation/salvation is *not* separable from "hope." Notice also that "hope" is associated with the mind ("helmet") whereas "faith and love" are associated with the heart ("breastplate"). We see that this distinction is most relevant as we look further for a scriptural definition of "hope." "Hope" is defined two ways:

1. Hope: the mystery of God, which is Christ in you ("you" is plural = church), the hope of glory (Colossians 1:27).

Almost immediately following (Col. 2:1), there is an explicit prayer for Laodicea, the only one of the seven churches in Revelation 2–3 that, in addition to Ephesus, is mentioned in Paul's epistles. This prayer is for the "full assurance of understanding of the mystery of God, and of the Father, and of Christ, in whom are hidden all the treasures of wisdom and knowledge... Beware lest any man spoil you through philosophy and vain deceit, after the tradition of men, after the rudiments ("one of a row or series") of the world, and not after Christ... Let no man, therefore, judge you in food, or in drink, or in respect of a feast day, or of the new moon, or of a sabbath, which are a shadow of things to come; but the body is of Christ... Why, as though living in the world, are you subject to ordinances?... These things have indeed a show of wisdom in will-worship, and humility, and neglecting of the body, but [are] not of any honor [except] to the satisfying of the flesh..." (Col. 2:2–3, 8, 16, 20, 23)

In other words, *do not be deceived into believing that there is virtue in the knowledge of good and evil.*

Instead, if you are risen with Christ, seek those things that are above. Your life is hidden with Christ in God; when Christ, who is our life, shall appear (*phaneroo*), then shall you also appear (*phaneroo*) with him in glory (Colossians 3:1, 3–4).

Therefore, hope is a full understanding by the mind of the mystery of God, which is Christ in the church, which is Christ in you!

2. Hope: "When He shall appear ['phaneroo'], we shall be like Him; for we shall see Him as He is. Every man that has this hope in Him purifies himself even as He is pure" (1 John 3:2–3).

Compare:

"Then shall the righteous shine forth as the sun in the Kingdom of their Father. Who has ears to hear, let him hear" (Matt. 13:43).

See also, Revelation 13:8–10: Hope is associated with being written in the Lamb's Book of Life, knowing that Satan, who now overcomes the saints, will himself be overcome.

"They that be wise shall shine like the brightness of the firmament; and they that turn many to righteousness, as the stars forever and ever" (Dan. 12:3). (The "wise" are those who "understand what the will of the Lord is" [Eph. 5:17]).

"Unto you that fear my name shall the Sun of righteousness arise with healing in his wings" (Mal. 4:2).

"Denying ungodliness and worldly lusts... Looking for that blessed hope, and the glorious appearing ['epiphaneia'] of the great God and our Savior, Jesus Christ..." (Titus 2:12–14).

"The Lord shall... Destroy the Lawless One with the brightness ['epiphaneia'] of His coming ['parousia']" (2 Thess. 2:8).

Note that "hope" is both (1) present and (2) future. Hope belongs to the righteous who understand the will of the Lord and who fear His name, such that they deny all that is not of God, which is to deny worldly lusts. When we lose hope, we open ourselves to The Lie; or have we already begun believing The Lie? Recall again that, whereas faith and love are matters of the heart, hope is associated with the mind. We are not any longer conformed to this world only when we have been transformed by the renewing of the mind (Romans 12:2). Hence, the importance of Paul's prayer that there be "full assurance of understanding of the mystery of God." This mystery is uniquely related to understanding of the Father and of Christ (Col 2:2). As we will see later, it is at this very issue where "Antichrist attacks" (1 John 2:22). Without right understanding of Christ and His relationship to the Father, there is no hope.

It is necessary, now, for us to look more closely at 2 Thessalonians 2. As we go, continue to refer back and to compare with what has already been said. This you must do for yourself. Only as you are open to the leading of the Holy Spirit will you begin to comprehend the breadth and depth of "The Lie," which has so totally captivated the church system and many born-again believers.

Oneness Unto Jesus Christ—Basis of Hope—From Which "The Lie" Detracts

Let us begin with 2 Thessalonians 2:1 where Paul appeals to the hope (that is, the "coming"—"presence"—*parousia*) of our Lord Jesus Christ and "our gathering together *unto Him*" (emphasis added). Some believe that this refers to the rapture, and to the extent that *parousia* and rapture may be equivalent, this is surely one aspect of "our gathering together unto Him."

However, the Greek word for "gathering together" (*episunagogee*) is used only one other place in Scripture—Hebrews 10:25—where it is used in the admonition that we should not forsake the "gathering together" of ourselves as we see the day approaching. The prefix *epi,* which means literally "in the same place," can be interpreted to lay stress on the "place" where the gathering together shall occur, or on the "unto" of the gathering together. The "unto" is Christ!

The verb *sunago,* which means "gather together" without the stress of the "unto," has seven New Testament usages:

1–2. "Jerusalem, Jerusalem, you that kill prophets. How often I would have gathered together your children even as a hen gathers together her chickens under her wing" (Matt. 23:37).

3. "He shall send His angels with a great sound of a trumpet and they shall gather together His elect from the four winds" (Matt. 24:31).

4. "All the city was gathered together at the door [unto Jesus]" (Mark 1:33).

5. "Then shall He send His angels, and shall gather together His elect from the four winds" (Mark 13:27).

6. "When there were gathered together an innumerable multitude of people [unto Jesus] ... He began to say unto His disciples, first of all, 'Beware of the leaven of the Pharisees, which is hypocrisy ... For a man's life consists not in the abundance of the things which he possesses" (Luke 12:1, 15).

7. "O Jerusalem, Jerusalem, which kills the prophets ... how often I would have gathered together your children ... " (Luke 13:34).

Paul is pleading with Christians to maintain their oneness. This oneness only exists when our "gathering together" is unto the Lord Jesus Christ. Any other basis, or reason, for "gathering together" is fallacious.

We know from the story of the church at Ephesus (Rev. 2:4 with Acts 20:30 and 3 John 9) that division occurred, and is still occurring, in the church because men draw disciples after themselves. Paul, in associating the *parousia* and "our gathering together unto Him" (compare also to Genesis 49:10), makes it clear that oneness associated with the hope is the antidote to "being shaken in mind and troubled." When hope is neglected, forgotten, or lost, oneness dissipates, and then, in 2 Thessalonians 2:3, there is "falling away."

Falling Away Precedes Lawlessness and Ruin

The Greek word for "falling away" is *apostasia* from which we get the English word "apostasy." The word was used in secular Greek writings to describe political rebels. It is translated in Acts 21:21 as "forsake" in "to forsake Moses." The noun form, *apostasion,* is very significant because it is translated in Matthew 5:31; 19:7; and Mark 10:4 as "divorcement" which Jesus ascribes to "hardness of heart."[3]

As the heart hardens, it no longer qualifies as "fleshy tables of the heart" (2 Cor. 3:3). When the Holy Spirit cannot speak directly to our hearts, there is no choice but to lean instead on knowledge of good and evil.

In fact, all rebellion against God and His Word, from Lucifer to Eve, to Korah, to the Pharisees, to modern-day Laodicean Christians, is political, for all disobedience is against the rule of the Kingdom of God (which is not food and drink, but righteousness and peace and joy in the Holy Spirit [Rom. 14:17]). Disobedience is "rule by self" rather than submission to the will of God. Rebellion is called the "sin of witchcraft" (1 Sam. 15:23) because, implicitly, to rebel against God is to assert that "I am as God and am capable of ruling myself." This opinion, you will recall, is integral to "The Lie."

When the rule and order of God are rejected, when His very paternity is rejected, then there is "lawlessness," and where there is "lawlessness," there is "ruin."

Man of Lawlessness, Son of Ruin Is the Antichrist

In the King James Translation, 2 Thessalonians 2:3–4 reads as follows (emphasis added):

> Let no man deceive you by any means; for [*that day shall not come*], except there come a [lit. the] falling away first,

> and that man of sin be revealed, the son of perdition, who opposes and exalts himself above all that is called God...as God, sits in the temple of God, showing himself that he is God.

First off, note that the words in italics in the King James Version ("that day shall not come") are not in the Greek text. A clearer sense is that the man of sin will not be revealed unless there is a falling away first. When, however, the falling away occurs, a false God will sit in the temple. This false God is the "man of sin" (better translated "man of lawlessness"), the "son of perdition" (or "son of ruin," or "ruined son").

Let's work backwards. What is the "temple of God"? Literally, the "temple" is *naos,* or the innermost sanctuary, the holy of holies, where God dwelt between the cherubim. In the New Testament record there appear to be six "temples":

1. The literal, physical building in Jerusalem that was the center of Jewish worship (Matt. 4:5; 27:51).
2. Jesus' body (John 2:19, 21).
3. An individual believer's body as the temple of the Holy Spirit (1 Cor. 3:16–17; 6:19).
4. Believers, collectively, as the habitation of God (2 Cor. 6:16; Eph. 2:21,22; Rev. 3:12).
5. Temple of God in heaven (Rev. 11:1, 19).
6. Lord God Almighty and the Lamb (Rev. 21:22).

The number "six" is not a good number in Scripture. It is the number of man. If we remove the physical building from the list, the next three references correspond perfectly to the scriptural meaning, or symbolism, of the numbers "1," "2," and "3"; that is, Jesus' body (1. beginning or source); individual believer's body (2. Witness, process, separation from world); believers collectively as the habitation of God, which is a work of the Holy Spirit (3. Divine perfection, a work of the Holy Spirit).

Those who opt for the physical building as the meaning here believe "The Lie," which both exalts the work of man's hands, and asserts that true believers (that is, born-again persons) cannot be deceived.

It is not Jesus' body, for Satan had no hold on Him (John 14:30). Similarly, it cannot be the temple of God in heaven, nor the Lord God Almighty and the Lamb. Hence, the "temple" here refers to believers, whether individually or collectively—most probably the latter. Such can only be the case if the individuals, the believers, have been deceived.

Contrast two passages as we begin to consider the "man of lawlessness" and the "son of ruin."

> For there is one God, and one mediator between God and men, the man, Christ Jesus.
>
> —1 Timothy 2:15

(Compare to 1 Peter 2:9, "You are a royal priesthood,")

> Thus says Jehovah God: "because your heart is lifted up, and you have said, I am a God, I sit in the seat of God, in the midst of the seas [humanity], yet you are a man, and not God, though you set your heart as the heart of God."
>
> —Ezekiel 28:2

With respect to this man described in Ezekiel 28, God concedes that this usurper has:

Wisdom and understanding (Ezek. 28:3–4:12)

Riches (Ezek. 28:4)

Merchandise (Ezek. 28:5)

Perfect beauty (Ezek. 28:12)

Anointing by God (Ezek. 28:14)

Has been in the realm of God's glory (i.e., midst of the stones of fire [compare to Exod. 24:10, 17]) (Ezek. 28:14)

God judges this usurper as profane because of:

Violence (Ezek. 28:16)

Sin (Ezek. 28:16)

Pride because of beauty (Ezek. 28:17)

Corrupted wisdom (Ezek. 28:17)

Defiled sanctuaries by merchandise (Ezek. 28:18)

There is throughout Scripture a fundamental concept of the "corporate" man. For example, the man Israel stands for all his children, and the sons together are known as Israel. Adam stands for all men; and, together, all natural men are Adam. Christ alone stands for all men who are risen with Him into new life, for we are part of Him—He is the Head, we are the body—Christ is one corporate man.

From the passage we have just read in 1 Timothy, we see that there is only one mediator, one priest, between God and man. Yet, in Christ Jesus we are all a royal priesthood, a single corporate priest so long as we dwell in unity (Ps. 133). We (plural) are the priest (singular) for the whole world after the order of Melchizedek.

Satan is likewise a corporate being—He is the head, even as Christ. His children, all those who love self more than God, constitute his corporate being. Hence in reading Ezekiel 28 it is never totally clear whether the reference is to a human king of Tyre, a satanic being known as the Prince of Tyre, or Lucifer himself. If you can grasp the concept of corporicity, you see it doesn't matter, for they are all the same. They are one being in Antichrist, even as born-again believers are one in Christ.

Earlier, when we were looking into Revelation 14, we saw reference to the "beast and his image." "Image" literally means "likeness," "representation," or "manifestation." For example, in Colossians 1:15, the "image of the invisible God" suggests that Christ is the visible representation and manifestation of God. What we see here is this same concept. The "image" and the "beast" are one corporate spiritual being even as Christ and His church are One—with the church purposed to manifest God on earth (John 17:21). Similarly, Jesus lumped the Pharisees as one with their "Father the Devil" (John 8:44) whom they manifested on earth!

This is certainly, and clearly, the case with the Antichrist Christ. In 1 John 2:18, John says, "You have heard that Antichrist [singular] shall come, even now there are many Antichrists [plural]." *Antichrist* is then defined as "they who went out from us." Once more we see the thought that to be in Christ is to be gathered, as One, unto Him; *where there is separation, there is Antichrist*; John then states that The Lie is associated with Antichrist, and *Antichrist* is more explicitly defined:

> He is Antichrist, that denies the Father and the Son.
>
> —1 JOHN 2:22

The seduction associated with "The Lie" involves our not continuing "in the Son and in the Father" (1 John 2:24). This clearly indicates that "continuing in the Son" involves an identification which was already being lost. What is this "continuing in the Son"? In 1 John 2:27 we see that The truth, the opposite of The Lie, is to "abide in Him." What is this "abiding in Him"?

The result of "continuing in the Son," or "abiding in Him," is given clearly:

> "Abide in Him that:
> When He shall appear [*phaneroo*],
> we may have confidence...
> At His coming [*parousia*]
> we may not be ashamed" (1 John 2:28).
> "...He is righteous...
> Everyone that does righteousness
> is born of Him" (1 John 2:29).

The result of abiding, or continuing, in the Son is righteousness that we may rejoice in His *parousia.*

Let us now study the meaning of "man of lawlessness," the "ruined son." As we look at these terms, it is important to keep in mind that these are not necessarily one specific person, but rather are more easily understood as a corporate spiritual being who seeks to usurp the place of Christ in the midst of believers, the corporate church; and in their hearts as individuals.

Lawlessness vs. Righteousness

As we consider the "man of lawlessness," let there be no doubt that He is Antichrist. Bible numerics affirm this. The numerical value of "man of lawlessness, "son of ruin," is "666 x 6"! The numerical value of 2 Thessalonians 2:3–4 is "666 x 22." Second Thessalonians 2:8 ("Then the Lawless One will be revealed whom the Lord will consume with the Spirit of His mouth") has a value of "666 x 13." The "power and signs and wonders" He performs (2 Thess. 2:9) are "666 x 6."[4]

The word *lawlessness* appears twice in 2 Thessalonians 2—"man of lawlessness" (v. 3) and "mystery of lawlessness" (v. 7). The related adjective *lawless* is used in verse 8 (KJV—"wicked one").

In doing a word study of *lawlessness* one is struck by the somewhat different emphases that appear from its use in Paul's epistles as compared with its use by Jesus in the gospels. In Paul's epistles it is clear that "lawlessness" is sin, or unrighteousness.

Rom. 6:19	**"Servants to uncleanness and to lawlessness, unto lawlessness"**	**vs.**	**"Servants to righteousness, unto holiness"**
2 Cor. 6:14	**"Lawlessness . . . Darkness"**	**vs.**	**"Righteousness . . . Light"**
Heb. 1:9	**"Hated lawlessness"**	=	**"Loved righteousness"**
Heb. 10:17	**"Lawlessness"**	=	**"Sins"**
1 John 3:4	**"Transgression of the law" (lit. lawlessness)**	=	**"Commits sin"**
Matt. 7:21–23	**"You that work lawlessness" (v. 23)**	=	**(*not*) "doing will of Father in heaven" (v. 21)**

Thus "lawlessness" deprives of Sonship (2 Cor. 6:14) and leads to death (Rom. 6:19), whereas righteousness results in life (Rom. 6:19), Sonship (2 Cor. 6:14; 1 John 3:10), anointing with the oil of gladness (Heb. 1:9), and the promise that we shall be like Him as He is when He shall appear (1 John 3:3–4).

It is important to know who are the lawless ones referred to in these verses. Where do we find them? For the answer, let us turn to the words of Jesus.

Matt. 7:21–23	WHO: Prophesied in Jesus' name Cast out demons in Jesus' name Has done many wonderful works in Jesus' name
	JUDGMENT: You who work lawlessness (KJV—"iniquity"), depart from Me, I never knew you.
Matt. 13:41	WHO: All things in His Kingdom that offend
	JUDGMENT: Those who do lawlessness (KJV—"iniquity") shall be gathered out of the Kingdom.
Matt. 23:28	WHO: Outwardly appear righteous unto men
	JUDGMENT: You are full of hypocrisy and lawlessness (KJV—"iniquity"). You are witnesses against yourselves (v. 31) that you are sons of them who killed the prophets; how can you escape the damnation of hell?
Matt. 24:5, 11–12	WHO: Many shall come in my name, saying "I am Christ" (that is, saying "I am part of the corporate Christ of Ephesians 1:22–23.") Many false prophets shall arise and deceive many.
	JUDGMENT: Because lawlessness (KJV—"iniquity") shall abound, love (*agape*—i.e., God-given love) of many shall grow cold. This is the abomination of desolation spoken of by Daniel the prophet (v. 15).

These are your friends and mine, in the Kingdom, ministering in the name of Jesus. This could be you. Let us have an ear to hear what the Spirit is speaking to our hearts.

What is "lawlessness"? It is to be outside the law—the law of Christ, the law of love. The law of love is obedience to the will of the Father. See 1 Corinthians 9:19–21 and Galatians 5:13–14, 6:2, and then compare with Hebrews 5:5–10 and Philippians 2:7. In lawlessness, that is in disobedience to the will of God, we identify with darkness, Belial ("worthlessness"), unbelief, and idolatry, denying that we are the people of God in whom He will dwell—this is true even though we are born again and thereby are designated as the temple of the living God (2 Cor. 6:14–18).

The "man of lawlessness" is that corporate being who denies God's will and authority even as He claims to serve, and, in fact, does minister in His name. The antithesis of the corporate "Man of Lawlessness" is the corporate Melchizedek, the "King of Righteousness" (Heb. 7:1–2). We see this antithesis even in Bible numerics.[5] Whereas the "Man of Lawlessness" is associated with "666," Melchizedek is associated with "888." For example, the original Melchizedek, King of Salem, priest of the Most High God (Heb. 7:1) is "888 x 6." In Hebrews 7:17 and 6:20 we see "888 x 5" and "888 x 7," respectively. Compare for emphasis these additional expressions:

1 x 888—"I am Jehovah, I change not" (Mal. 3:6)

2 x 888—"The Lamb in the midst of the throne" (Rev. 7:17)

3 x 888—"Following the Lamb" (Rev. 14:4)

4 x 888—"To a meeting with the Bridegroom" (Matt. 25:1)

5 x 888—"The Mediator, a man Christ Jesus" (1 Tim. 2:5)

5 x 888—"The first and the last, the beginning and the end" (Rev. 22:13)

6 x 888—"The one having given Himself on behalf of sins" (Gal. 1:4)

7 x 888—"For the Lord God Almighty and the Lamb are the Temple of it" (Rev. 21:22)

Revelation 1:5–6 makes it clear that God is establishing His church as a Kingdom of Priests. The forerunner (Heb. 6:20) is the man Jesus, our High Priest (Heb. 4:14). Then, note that in Hebrews 5:5, it is no longer "Jesus," but "Christ," the corporate son of man, who is identified as "priest forever after the order of Melchizedek." Herein is the fulfillment of Isaiah 59:16:

> And he saw that there was no man [singular] and wondered that there was no intercessor.

And the fulfillment of Isaiah 62:6–7:

> I have set watchmen [plural]... Which shall never hold their peace day nor night: you that are the Lord's remembrancers, keep not silence, and give Him no rest.

The man of lawlessness is against God's people and rebels against God's will, being a law unto himself. The ultimate expression of this lawlessness in the church is Laodicea, which means "sayings of the people," "people's opinions," or "people's rights." This contrasts with the unfallen Ephesus where all is focused around, and submitted to, the Headship of the Lord Jesus Christ.

The "Man of Lawlessness" shall be "revealed" (2 Thess. 2:3). The word *revealed* indicates something that is "uncovered" or "unveiled." Hence, the existence of the Man of Lawlessness in the midst of God's people shall not be recognized openly and generally until the time of the end (v. 8) when the Lord Himself shall "reveal" Him with the "brightness of His presence" (KJV—"coming" which is Greek *parousia*). In other words, the fiery glory of Christ (Head and body) will make plain the counterfeit, and destroy him.

For those who have eyes to see, the existence of the "man of lawlessness" can be seen in our midst even now. In this regard, the first five usages of this word "reveal" (Gk "apokalupto") are most instructive.

1. "Fear not Beelzebub ["Lord of the dwelling"] and his household, for there is nothing covered [*sunkalupto*—"to cover completely"] that shall not be revealed; and hidden, that shall not be known" (Matt. 10:26).

2. Jesus said, "[I thank you, Father, because] you have hidden these things from the wise and prudent, and have revealed them unto babes" (Matt. 11:25).

3. "To whomsoever the Son will reveal..." (Matt. 11:27).

4. "Flesh and blood have not revealed it unto you, but my Father who is in heaven" (Matt. 16:17).

5. "This child is... For a sign which shall be spoken against... That the thoughts of many hearts may be revealed." You will see when a "sword shall pierce through your own soul also" (Luke 2:34–35).

Need we say more? We will see if we want to see. Elsewhere Jesus said that it is the little children who shall enter the Kingdom of heaven. "Out of the mouths of babes [not the wise and prudent], God has perfected praise" (Matt. 21:16). Let him that has an ear, let him hear what the Spirit is saying to the churches!

Son of Ruin vs. Son of Man

The "Son of Ruin" (KJV—"son of perdition") opposes and exalts himself above all that is called God. The antithesis to the "Son of Ruin" is the "Son of Man." Put another way, we compare the "ruined son" with the "perfect son."

A little recognized fact is that Jesus Christ is called the Son of Man eigthy-eight times in the New Testament, compared with the forty-six times He is called the Son of God. Always, with respect to His first and Second Coming, all aspects of His ministry, and His suffering obedience, Jesus calls Himself the Son of Man (see Appendix B).

What is the meaning of "son"? The word *son,* in addition to natural descent, conveys an expression of one's nature, or what one is. For example, in 1 Samuel 25:17 the King James Version translates the Hebrew as "son of Belial" ("son of worthlessness"), whereas others translate the concept of nature more directly as "worthless fellow" or "worthless one." Psalms 8:4 and Hebrews 2:6 distinguish between "man" and "son of man," wherein the latter is associated with a visitation from God. Man was made in God's own image (Gen. 1:27). Man was commissioned to exercise dominion (Gen. 1:28) and to eat of the Tree of Life (Gen. 2:17). Man was intended as such a full expression of God's nature that he is called the "son of God" (Luke 3:38); it was God's intention, as the Word ("voice"), to visit him and to walk with him (Gen. 3:8).

All that God had purposed for man was brought to ruin when man was flattered by Satan into opposing God (compare to Proverbs 26:28 and Isaiah 3:8). The "first Adam" (lit. "first man"), therefore, fell from Sonship as an expression of the nature of God and became a ruined son. Hence, the necessity for the "second Adam" (lit. "second man"). In Jesus Christ we have not the image of the earthy (ruin), but the image of the heavenly (1 Corinthians 15:45–50). In Christ there is restoration of man as God had purposed him in the beginning—one in God's own image with whom He could visit—the Son of Man. (In 1 Corinthians 15, therefore, we see the fullest expression of corporicity, or representationalism, in that, in the sight of God, there are only two men: (1) the corporate first Adam, son of ruin, who opposes God (compare to Rom. 9:20; Isa. 45:9–10; Jer 18:4–6); and (2) the second Adam, son of man, who bears the image of the heavenly and is destined to inherit the Kingdom (1 Cor. 15:49–50).)

In other words, the first vessel made by the potter was ruined, so the potter made another vessel as it seemed good to the potter (Jer 18:4).

Let us consider more specifically the expression "son of ruin" (KJV—"son of perdition"). This is the Greek word *apolia* which has the same root as *Apollyon* ("destroyer" or "one who ruins"), which is one of the names of Satan, and who is identified as the angel of the "bottomless pit" (Rev. 9:11). *Bottomless* is also translated "deep" in Luke 8:31 and Romans 10:7, where it is clearly the opposite of heaven (compare to Rom. 10:6), a place of death. In Revelation 11:7 it is a source of opposition to the saints, and in Revelation 17:8 seems to indicate that ruin (perdition) occurs subsequent to his arising. While the exegesis is not totally clear, there is some evidence for believing that the bottomless, or deep, is synonymous with the sea of humanity. This may be confirmed by John 4:11–14 where *pit* is translated "well." Jesus says, "Whosoever drinks of the water from Jacob's well [*pit*; that is, natural life] shall thirst again. But whosoever drinks of the water that I shall give him shall never thirst, for the water that I shall give him shall be in him a well [not *pit*, but *fountain*] of water [that is, spiritual life] springing up into everlasting life."

The Son of Ruin, unlike the Son of Man (which is the corporate Christ) is the corporate opposer. What constitutes this opposition to our Creator? If we can see this clearly, we can know whether we are ruin, or are the image (reflection) of God. We could do a word study on *ruin* (KJV—*perdition*) or on *opposer* with equal results, but we shall examine here only the former.

Scripture Context	Ruin Is:	Result Is:
1. Matt. 7:13—"Wide is the gate, and broad is the way, that leads to ruin (KJV—*destruction*), and many there be who go in."	Broad (easy) way	Doesn't lead to life (Matt. 7:14)
2–3. Matt. 26:8; Mark 14:4—Woman poured precious ointment on Jesus' head. Disciples were indignant and said, "To what purpose is this ruin (KJV—*waste*)?" Jesus said, "She has wrought a good work."	Murmuring against a "good work"; i.e., a work that exalts Jesus even though it hinders the exaltation of man through a dead work. Concern with money	Work not remembered (Compare to 1 Cor. 3:11–15, esp. v. 13)

Scripture Context	Ruin Is:	Result Is:
4. John 17:12—"None is lost, but the son of ruin (KJV—*perdition*)...[rest] might have my joy fulfilled in themselves (v. 13)... world hates them, because they are not of the world (v. 14)"	Lack of oneness (v. 11)... world loves because part of the world; hence, one who loves the world. No joy	Lost* Not kept in His name (John 17:11)
*Note: *Lost* (which is the same word as in Matt. 18:11, "Son of Man is come to seek that which was lost") is *appollumi*, which means "totally or utterly ruined."		
5. Acts 8:20—"Thy money perish [lit. "be to ruin," or "be to destruction"] with you, because you thought that the gift of God may be purchased with money."	Belief that money can buy God's favor Heart is not right in the sight of God (v. 21) Gall of bitterness (v. 23) Bond of iniquity* (v. 23)	Need to repent and pray for forgiveness (Acts 8:22)
*Note: *Iniquity* here means "legal injustice," or "condition of not being right with authority."		

Scripture Context	Ruin Is:	Result Is:
6. Acts 25:16—"It is not the manner of the Romans to deliver any man to ruin [KJV—"to die"]" before he has met his accusers face to face.		Result is adverse judgment (Acts 25:15) "face to face" (compare to 1 John 2:28; 1 Cor. 13:12)
7. Rom. 9:22—"God . . . endured with much long suffering the vessels of wrath fitted to ruin (KJV—*destruction*)"	Hardened (v. 18) Resists God's will (v. 19) Replies against God (v. 20) Opposite of (v. 23) vessels of mercy Seeks righteousness by works of law, not by faith (v. 31–32)	Wrath or anger rather than mercy

Scripture Context	Ruin Is:	Result Is:
8. Phil. 1:27–28, 2:3—"Stand fast in one spirit, with one mind striving together for the faith of the gospel; in nothing terrified by your adversaries, which is to them an evident token of ruin (KJV—*perdition*), but to you of salvation . . . for unto you it is given . . . not only to believe in Him, but also to suffer for His sake . . . Let nothing be done through strife or vain glory, but in lowliness of mind let each esteem other better than themselves."	1. Not standing fast in one spirit 2. Not striving together 3. Terrified/afraid of adversaries 4. Disbelieving Christ 5. Unwilling to suffer 6. Working through strife and vain glory 7. Esteeming self better than others	To receive rebuke (Phil. 2:15) Same experience which will be salvation for some will be ruin for these (Phil. 1:28)

Scripture Context	Ruin Is:	Result Is:
9. Phil. 3:18–19—“Many walk… [as] enemies of the cross of Christ, whose end is ruin, whose God is their belly [appetite], and glory in their shame, who mind earthy things [forgetting that] our citizenship is in heaven.”	Enemies of the cross (i.e., not denying self, Matt. 16:24) because of: • Fleshly appetites • Concern with earthy things • Don’t comprehend that citizenship is in heaven Glory in their shame (in other words, that which God despises they consider to have religious merit; compare to Isa. 1:10–15, 1 Sam. 15:22; 2 Pet. 2:19–22, “The dog is turned to his own vomit again.”)	Paul weeps for them (Phil. 3:18)

Scripture Context	Ruin Is:	Result Is:
10. 2 Thess. 2:3—"Let no man deceive you . . . There come the falling away first, and that man of lawlessness be revealed, the son of ruin, who opposes and exalts himself above all that is called God."	Opposes God Exalts Self	Lord shall consume with Spirit of His mouth Lord shall destroy with brightness of His *parousia*
11. 1 Tim. 6:9–10—"They that will be rich fall into temptation and a snare, and many foolish and hurtful lusts, which drown men in destruction and ruin (KJV—*perdition*). For the love of money is the root of all evil, which, while some coveted after, they have erred from the faith, and pierced themselves through with many sorrows."	Proud (1 Tim. 6:4) Disputing over words (1 Tim. 6:4) Discontented (1 Tim. 6:6–8) Desire to be rich (1 Tim. 6:9) (compare to Rev. 3:17) Love of money (1 Tim. 6:9–10) *Not* loving, patient, or meek	Many sorrows

Scripture Context	Ruin Is:	Result Is:
12. Heb. 10:35–39—"Cast not away... your confidence, which has great recompense of reward. For you have need of patience that, after you have done the will of God, you might receive the promise... Live by faith (lit. "by the faithfulness of God"); but if any draw back, my soul shall have no pleasure in him. But we are not of them who draw back unto ruin (KJV—*perdition*), but of them that believe unto the saving of the soul."	Not having confidence that God is faithful* Impatient with God Drawing back from dependence on God	*Not* receiving the reward (Heb. 10:35)
*Note: "The just shall live by His [that is, God's] faithfulness" (Habakkuk 2:4). When we doubt God (as Eve), disobey His will (as Korah or Saul), or fall from first love (as church at Ephesus), it is the effect or result of not believing that God is faithful to perform His promise(s).		

13–16. 2 Pet. 2:1–3—“But there were false prophets also among the people, even as there shall be false teachers among you, who secretly shall bring in ruinous (KJV—*destructive*) heresies, even denying the Lord that bought them, and bring upon themselves swift ruin (KJV—*destruction*). And many shall follow their ruinous (KJV—*pernicious*) ways, by reason of whom the ways of truth shall be evil spoken of. And through covetousness shall they, with feigned words, make merchandise of you; whose judgment now for a long time lingers not, and their ruin (KJV—*damnation*) slumbers not.”	False teachers (2 Pet. 2:1) Denying the Lord (2 Pet. 2:1) Speak evil of the truth (hence, to promote The Lie) Covetous Make merchandise of the people of God (compare Rev. 18:11) Walk after the flesh (2 Pet. 2:10) Despise government (hence, lawless) (2 Pet. 2:10) Presumptuous (2 Pet. 2:10) Self-willed (2 Pet. 2:10) Speak evil of dignities (dignities = *doxa*, glory)* (2 Pet. 2:10) Speak evil of things they understand not Following way of Balaam who loved wages of unrighteousness (2 Pet. 2:15) Promise liberty, but bring into bondage (2 Pet. 2:19)	Chains of darkness (2 Pet. 2:4) Reserved unto the day of judgment to be punished (2 Pet. 2:9) Shall receive reward of unrighteousness (2 Pet. 2:13) To whom mist of darkness is reserved forever (2 Pet. 2:17) Better for them not to have known the way of righteousness (2 Pet. 2:21)

Scripture Context	Ruin Is:	Result Is:
*Note: In comparing Phil. 3:18–19, we see that the "man of ruin" glories in that which is shame in the sight of God, and speaks evil, as of shame, of that which is glory in the sight of God. Jesus, the Son of Man, rather found glory in that which man sees as shame (Phil. 2:7; Heb. 12:2). A similar thought is contained in 1 Cor. 1:23–2:16, where that which appears to men as folly or foolishness is seen by God as wisdom, and vice versa.		
17. 2 Pet. 3:7—Men doubt that the Lord is coming again because He has tarried so long. But recall this, that the heavens and the earth are reserved "unto fire against the day of judgment and ruin (KJV—*perdition*) of ungodly men . . . Be not ignorant of this one thing, that one day is with the Lord as a thousand years . . ."* "Be diligent that you may be found of Him in peace, without spot, and blameless" (2 Pet. 3:14).	Doubt the reality of the Lord's coming/*parousia*; that is, men may believe, or claim to believe, He is coming, but by their love of the world they testify otherwise.	Reserved unto fire Will be found spotted and full of blame

Scripture Context	Ruin Is:	Result Is:
*Note: There is a specific time element associated with the consummation of ruin. There is reason to believe that, given God's consistency, the duration of the world will be one week of seven days, or seven thousand years beginning with Adam. Biblical chronology, based on genealogical time references within the Scriptures themselves, ascribes about 4,000 years from Adam to Christ; and, we have completed about 2,000 years since that time—for a total of six thousand years, the number of Man ("6"). If the seventh day of 1,000 years will be a Sabbath rest (the so-called Millenium), then clearly it is time for Christians seriously to consider whether they will be found "without spot and blameless."		
18. 2 Pet. 3:16–17—The unlearned and unstable wrest Paul's teaching and also the other Scriptures "unto their own ruin [KJV—*destruction*] . . . Beware lest you also, being led away with the error of the wicked, fall from your own steadfastness."	Wrest/twist the Scriptures	Fall from steadfastness

Scripture Context	Ruin Is:	Result Is:
19–20. Rev. 17:8,11—"The beast that saw was, and is not, and shall ascend out of the bottomless pit, and go into ruin [KJV—*perdition*] and the beast that was, and is not, even he is the eighth* [king], and is of the seven, and goes into ruin."	Make war with the Lamb (Rev. 17:14; 11:7–8)	Lamb shall overcome them together with the called, and chosen and faithful (Rev. 17:14)
*Note: "Eight" is the number of "new beginnings," or "new order." This signifies, therefore, a new order, or different kind, of king.		

These verses, containing the twenty New Testament references to "ruin," are not new to any of us. However, they have been read in the past by those to whom they apply without recognition, or comprehension, that these Scriptures convict most Christians, and especially Christian leadership, of sin and of the need for repentance. May it not be so with those who read these pages. Let us rather start from the premise that they apply to all of us and determine, rather, to seek the light of life that we might find the way of deliverance.

Let us not look to these descriptions of the "man of ruin" as knowledge of good and evil to make us spiritually wise, but rather let us be willing to be led by the Spirit into life and ministry that is pleasing and acceptable to the Lord Jesus Christ. The following characteristics associated with "ruin" should be particularly noted from these twenty usages.

The way to "ruin," to mar that which God has purposed, is easy—it is a "broad way." This being the first reference (the place of "beginnings"), it is most significant. The object of Jesus' teaching in Matthew 7:13 was not the world, but his disciples (Matt. 5:1-2). He is warning us, as His disciples, that it is likely that we will find ourselves on this road! It is even more likely that we will find it comfortable and pleasant, or easy, or logical, perhaps even inevitable!

The most prevalent characteristic (usages 2, 3, 8, 11, 13–16, 18, 19–20) associated with "ruin" is disagreement, fighting, or striving with other Christians. The second most prevalent characteristic, which is most likely, in some sense, causative of the former, is the love of, or concern about, money, wherein God's people are treated like merchandise (usages 2, 3, 5, 11, 13–16, and, probably, 19–20).

The "son of ruin" was, prior to Christ; and is not, at the time when the church was still in "first love"; and, is to come, when the church falls from "first love." From Revelation 3:6, 3 John 9, and Acts 20:30, 33–35, we see that this fall is directly associated with the desire of elders and teachers to draw men after themselves rather than to Christ; and, the beginnings of the management of the church as a business which, at the time of judgment, even as at this present hour, will be the principal characteristic of the church (Rev. 18:11–19; compare to John 2:16–17, Luke 19:45–48, Proverbs 3:13–18, and Isaiah 1:23). It is with this in view, I believe, that Paul attributes disorderliness to those who eat another's bread. Paul, himself, set the example of working even as he ministered. Could it be that "if any would not work, neither should he eat" applies to the ministry rather than to "street bums"? (2 Thess. 3:6–12) (Note: While Paul acknowledges the "right" of the ministry under the law to "sow" spiritual and thereby to "reap" carnal (1 Cor. 9:1–11), he himself submits to the higher law of love: "Nevertheless, we have not used this right, but bear all things, *lest we should hinder the gospel of Christ*" (1 Cor. 9:12–19).)

The emphasis on money in the church is symptomatic of deeper problems such as "loving the world," "exalting man and his methods," and, most grievous of all, "doubting the faithfulness of God."

This brings us to specific consideration of the "Son of Ruin,"[1] a term used in John 17:12 with reference to Judas Iscariot. His name is most instructive:

JUDAS: "he shall be praised"

ISCARIOT: "he will be hired"

In his names we see the exaltation/praise of man, and the fact that he is hired. Hence, his identity with the Son of Ruin characteristics is affirmed.

---

[1]KJV: "Son of Perdition."

The consequences identified with "ruin," such as receiving rebuke (#8), being denied reward (#12), darkness forever (#13–16), reserved unto fire (#17), and even "lost" (#4) will cause many of us to dismiss the warnings as applicable only to the unsaved. In my view, we need not conclusively determine whether the Son of Ruin has been truly born again. It is enough to believe that we can be deceived. Does it matter whether we have been deceived into believing that man cannot lose his salvation, or that we have been deceived into believing that we are saved when we are not? Notwithstanding, let us not dismiss lightly Jesus' admonition that the elect can be deceived (Matt. 24:24), or Paul's concern that he himself could be a "castaway," meaning "reprobate" or "disapproved" (1 Cor. 9:27). And, as we have already seen, 2 Thessalonians 2:3 speaks of "falling away," 2 Peter 3:17 of "fall from your own steadfastness," and Revelation 2:4, "You have left your first love."

There are many types of Judas Iscariot, the Son of Ruin, or Ruined Son, in the Old Testament. Not the least of these was the creation of the golden calf as recorded in Exodus 32 and Acts 7:39–42. It was less than three months (Exodus 19:1) after the children of Israel had crossed the Red Sea, having been baptized in water and Spirit (1 Cor. 10:2), and still feeding on spiritual food (1 Cor. 10:3), that:

1. They complained that Moses had not yet come down out of the mount—they doubted he would ever come back (Exod. 32:1; Acts 7:40).

2. "The people gathered themselves together unto Aaron," (a man) (Exod. 32:1).

3. Aaron asks them for money (Exod. 32:2).

4. "All the people broke off the golden earrings which were in their ears, and brought them unto Aaron" (Exod. 32:3).

Note: Is this symbolic that they had ceased to hear? Compare:

"Would not obey him that was in the church in the wilderness" (Acts 7:38–39).

"In their hearts [the church] turned back again into Egypt" (Acts 7:39).

5. Aaron "made a melted calf" (Exod. 32:4).

6. Aaron built an altar before the calf... And said, "Tomorrow is a feast to Jehovah" (Exod. 32:5).

7. The people "rejoiced in the work of their own hands" (Acts 7:41).
   The people "sat down to eat, and to drink, and rose up to play" (Exod. 32:6).

8. "People... have corrupted themselves" (Exod. 32:7).

9. God said, "I will consume them" (Exod. 32:10).

10. Moses interceded to spare the people from God's wrath (Exod. 32:11–14, 30–35).

These people were God's people. They were born again unto salvation as they were delivered from the political and religious bondage of Egypt while passing through the Red Sea. Moses and Aaron were both God's anointed, but one led the people to God (as representative of the Son of Man), and the other gave them a calf (as representative of the Son of Ruin).

One more Old Testament example: Israel consisted of twelve sons, twelve tribes. Their names were taken before the presence of God on the body of the High Priest. On his shoulders their names were listed in birth order (Exod. 28:10), and on the breastplate of righteousness they were listed in spiritual order, reflecting a spiritual judgment. For example, Judah was born fourth, but was listed first in the spiritual order.

The sixth one born (representative of man) was Naphtali. He fell six positions, the most of any, to be listed last in the spiritual order. Moreover, on the breastplate of righteousness each tribe was represented by a gemstone (Exod. 28:17–20). The upper (most spiritual) gemstones were transparent and sparkling; the lesser gemstones were translucent, letting light through, but not sparkling; the twelfth, a jasper, identified with Naphtali, was opaque—letting no light through.

Naphtali, which means "my wrestling," reflected his mother Rachel's ("lamb's") striving with her sister: "With great wrestlings I have wrestled with my sister, and I have prevailed." Yet, really, she had not prevailed at all! Her own womb was still closed! Her methods, though she was a "lamb," were her own, and not of God. Naphtali's real mother was Bilhad, meaning "languishing" or "in decrepitude." Her other son was Dan, meaning "judging." Dan led the people of God into idolatry.

Once more we see the result when one of God's people (a "lamb"), being impatient, takes matters into her own hands. Where there is decrepitude, there has been a falling away. The result is ruin. Where there is judging and criticizing, there is idolatry.

Just as with Naphtali and Aaron, Judas Iscariot was one of Jesus' own, given him by God (John 17:12). Judas Iscariot had "power against unclean spirits, to cast them out, and to heal all manner of sickness and all manner of disease" (Matt. 10:1–4).

Judas Iscariot "fell" from "ministry and apostleship" by transgression that "he might go to his own place" (Acts 1:17, 25).

Judas Iscariot was more concerned with money than with worshipping Jesus (John 12:4–6).

Judas Iscariot, one of Jesus' own, gave entrance to Satan (Luke 22:3; John 13:2).

Judas Iscariot bargained with the high priests (representing Judaism) and sold out for money (Matt. 26:14).

Judas Iscariot was a friend of Jesus, and was not initially recognized, even by Jesus, as the traitor (Ps. 41:9, with John 13:18–19).

Judas Iscariot ate and fellowshipped with Jesus, and even had his feet washed by Jesus, but then went out at night to betray Him (John 13:2, 5, 26, 30).

Until the actual betrayal, no one but Jesus knew that Judas Iscariot had a heart that was different from the other disciples (John 13:28–29).

Until the very last, Judas Iscariot made a profession of loving Jesus, and accomplished the betrayal with a kiss (Luke 22:47; compare to Ps. 109:2–8). The kiss was a symbol of trust (Ps. 2:12)!

Judas Iscariot "stood with them" who were against Christ (John 18:5) at the moment of revelation, when Jesus revealed His presence as the "I AM." Previously, Jesus had been careful not to reveal Himself as the "I AM." As the revealing occurred ("I Am"), those who stood against Him, including Judas, fell to the ground (John 18:6). Even thus, shall "Antichrist" be destroyed "with the brightness of His *parousia*" (2 Thess. 2:8).

It would have been better for Judas Iscariot if he had never been born (Mark 14:18). Might it also be better for some if they had never been "born again"? (Heb. 6:4-8; 10:29–31, 39)

Where is the Son of Ruin, the Ruined Son? In the chapter under study, 2 Thessalonians 2, we see that "He who opposes and exalts himself above all that is called God, or that is worshipped, sits as God in the temple of God, showing Himself that he is God." That this opposer is within the church of Jesus Christ, the body of believers, there can be no doubt.

One additional confirmation of the seriousness of this matter appears from examination of the Greek word translated in 2 Thessalonians 2:4 as "exalts himself." This Greek word (*huperairomai*) is used only two additional places in the New Testament, and both are in 2 Corinthians 12:7 where Paul speaks of himself:

> And lest I should be exalted above measure through the abundance of the revelations [which God has given me], there was given to me a thorn in the flesh, the messenger of Satan to buffet me, lest I should be exalted above measure.

The message of Paul here is that a servant of the living God is to be "weak" (vv. 9–10)—for only then does the "power of Christ" become evident (v. 9). Such is the "Son of Man" in whom strength is made perfect in weakness as contrasted to the "Son of Ruin" in whom weakness is made perfect in strength!

The Son of Ruin shows Himself as God. The Son of Man never (and does not now) claimed to be God. This may startle you, but it is true. In the classic passage cited to demonstrate that Jesus claimed to be God, or at least to be equal with God (John 5:17–43), it is the Pharisees who assert that Jesus is "making himself equal to God." Do not believe the Pharisees, for they did not have light. Rather, Philippians 2:6 states, in literal translation, that Jesus "thought it not a thing to be held on to, to be equal with God, but emptied himself, and took upon himself the form of a servant, and was made in the likeness of men."

There is no evidence that Jesus even knew that He was the Son of God[1] prior to hearing the voice of God declare at His baptism: "You are my beloved Son; in you I am well pleased" (Luke 3:22). Then, immediately, the scriptural narrative is interrupted to trace Jesus' natural descent back to Adam/Man "of God" (Luke 3:38). It is this point, Jesus' Sonship, concerning which Satan raises doubt in the wilderness: "If you be the Son of God?" (Luke 4:3, 9)

Clearly, in John 5:17–20, and elsewhere, Jesus claims only to be the "son of God." This distinction is important, and is essen-

---

[1] Some will point to Mary's knowledge (Luke 1:35), but it appears that she kept this in her heart as a secret which she did not understand (Luke 2:19).

tial to seeing through "The Lie," because in 1 John 2:22–23 it is explicit that Antichrist will deny the father and son relationship. "Who is the liar but he that denies that Jesus is the Christ?" (1 John 2:22). "Christ" (Heb. *Messiah*) is the "Anointed One," the "son given" of Isaiah 9:6 and elsewhere. To claim that Jesus was God while on earth is to deny his "Christ-nature," and to deny the father and son relationship between God and the one whom He has anointed with the Holy Spirit. This anointing occurred when the voice of God identified Jesus as the beloved son at Jordan: "And Jesus, being full of the Holy Spirit, returned from Jordan, and was led by the Spirit into the wilderness... And, when the devil had ended all the testing... Jesus returned in the power of the Spirit into Galilee... And He came to Nazareth, where he had been brought up... And there was delivered unto him the Book of the prophet Isaiah, [from which He read]: 'The Spirit of the Lord is upon me, because He has anointed me to preach the gospel to the poor; he has sent me to heal the brokenhearted, to preach deliverance to the captives, and recovering of sight to the blind, to set at liberty them that are bruised, to preach the acceptable year of the Lord'... And He began to say unto them, 'This day is this Scripture fulfilled in your ears'" (Luke 4:1, 13–14,16–19, 21).

Jesus was not equal with God. He claimed only to be the Son of God upon whom rested the Holy Spirit. He is explicit that "the son can do nothing of himself" (John 5:19).

The Lie of the Pharisees (John 5:18), which has been perpetuated in Christian theology, is a major source, perhaps the major source, of weakness in the church. Why are we so weak when we have been given these tremendous statements of purpose?

- "As you [Father] have sent me into the world, even so also have I sent them into the world" (John 17:18).
- We are to be one in God even as Jesus was in the Father, and the Father in Him (John 17:21).

- We have the same glory the Father gave to Jesus (John 17:22).
- The same love the Father had for Jesus is in us (John 17:26).

There are other significant statements of purpose as well: "joint heirs with Jesus Christ," "we shall do greater works than Jesus," and on, and on!

We take lightly our commission and purpose because we consider that we are different than Jesus—we are "only human." After all, Jesus was God; we are man. *This is Antichrist doctrine.* Rather, the Scriptures are explicit that "as many as are *led by the Spirit of God,* they are the *sons of God*" (Rom. 8:14). In 2 Corinthians 6:16–18, the temple of God is clearly described as consisting of "sons of God"; and, again, in Hebrews 2:9–12 we are "sons" of God and "brothers" to Jesus.

In Romans 5:10 there is distinction made between our being "reconciled to God by the death of His son," and our being saved in His life (KJV—"saved by his life"). The latter is qualitatively "much more" than the former. This "life" is, of course, resurrection life, and refers to our Sonship.

Jesus was limited. He was not omniscient, nor omnipotent, in His incarnation.

> The Word was made *flesh* and dwelt among us.
>
> —JOHN 1:14

In John 8:26, Jesus says, "I speak to the world these things that I have heard of him [the Father]."

In John 17 Jesus takes credit for having overcome the world (John 16:33) on the basis of three narrow assignments:

1. "I have finished the work which you gave me to do" (John 17:4).

2. "I have manifested your name unto the [twelve] men you gave me out of the world" (John 17:6).

3. "I have given unto them the words which you gave me" (John 17:8).

The significance of all this is that we, you and I, dare not make the excuse, "I'm only human." In Christ, we can be, if we are "led by the Spirit of God" (that is, led by the Holy Spirit; Rom. 8:14), sons of God, and we can overcome the world! Why else would He *seven times* make promises to those who overcome? (See Revelation 2:7, 11, 17, 26; 3:5, 12, 21.) If we doubt that our calling is to be "perfect" (Eph. 4:13), then we doubt God and we thereby identify ourselves with the Son of Ruin.

The Spirit of God is known by those who confess that Jesus Christ is come in the flesh. Antichrist Christians confess *not* that Jesus Christ is come in the flesh (1 John 4:2–3).

> Many deceivers are entered into the world, who confess not that Jesus Christ comes in the flesh. This is the deceiver and the Antichrist. Look to yourselves, that we lose not those things which we have wrought, but that we receive a full reward. Whosoever transgresses, and abides not in the doctrine of Christ, has not God. He that abides in the doctrine of Christ, he has *both the Father and the Son.*
>
> —2 John 7–9, emphasis added

The Lie teaches us that we must have "knowledge of good and evil." The truth declares that we must feed upon the tree of life, which is the Son who has life in Himself (John 5:26). Jesus could speak "life" because the Father "dwells in me." Because He lives, we live (John 14:19). We live because Jesus is "in the Father," and we are "in Jesus" (John 14:20).

Throughout the Gospel of John there is clear indication of a handing down of life and truth from generation to generation (for example, John 15:15; 14:10–12, 23; 16:15). We are the forty-second generation from Abraham (Matt. 1:16–17).

> A seed shall serve Him; it shall be accounted to the Lord for a generation. They shall come and declare His righteousness unto a people that shall be born, that He has done this.

The foregoing quotation is from Psalm 22:30–31. Compare it with Isaiah 53:8, "Who shall declare His generation?" And with Isaiah 53:10, "He shall see His seed."

> We see Jesus, who was made a little lower than the angels for the suffering of death… For it became him, for whom are all things, and by whom are all things, in bringing many sons unto glory, to make the captain of their salvation perfect through sufferings…For both He that sanctifies and they who are sanctified are all of one, for which cause He is not ashamed to call them brothers…Behold I and the children whom God has given me…For verily He…took on the seed of Abraham. Wherefore, in all things it behooved Him to be made like his brothers, that he might be a merciful and faithful high priest in things to God, to make propitiation for the sins of the people…For in that He Himself has suffered being tempted, he is able to help them that are tempted.
>
> —Hebrews 2:9–11, 13, 16–18

It is a lie that we are something less than Jesus. We are the children of God, called to grow up into Sonship. You are not less than Jesus, for you are called to "follow His steps" who suffered for us, to do no sin (1 Pet. 2:21–22).

> Beloved, now are we the children (KJV—*sons*) of God, and it does not yet appear what we shall be, but we know that, when He shall appear, we shall be like Him, for we shall see Him as He is.
>
> —1 John 3:2

Now note 1 John 3:3: "And every man that has this hope in him purifies himself even as He is pure." Even as we stand, we should take heed lest we fall (1 Cor. 10:12), for the first Adam, too, was the "son of God" (Luke 3:38). If Adam fell from Sonship by believing The Lie, so might we. Of course, if we have already believed The Lie, we have already fallen; or perhaps because we have believed The Lie, we had never attained unto the status of a "son of God," which is our privilege in Christ as the Son of Man. Let us determine to exercise our full privileges of Sonship in Christ, for His grace is sufficient to restore us, or to bring us, even unto glory in Him.

Don't You Remember That I Told You These Things?

What a rebuke! Although they had been told all these things by Paul, they were destined to fall (2 Thess. 2:5).

The church at Ephesus had the privilege of an extended ministry by Paul. Paul had declared to them "all the counsel of God" (Acts 20:27). Paul warned them "everyone night and day with tears" (Acts 20:31) that men would seek to draw them away from Christ, yet they still left their "first love," even Christ (Rev. 2:4).

The truth is in your Bible! You need not that any man teach you; rather, the anointing of the Holy Spirit will teach you the truth as you read the Word and open your heart to Him (1 John 2:27).

You, too, have been told. Don't you remember? Haven't you seen? He that has an ear, let him hear what the Spirit is saying to the churches!

Holding Fast vs. Falling Away

Paul had explained to the Thessalonian Christians that the Man of Lawlessness would be revealed, and the Son of Ruin would claim equality with God, if there were a "falling away." However, in the verses before us (2 Thess. 2:6–7), Paul further explains that, even though the "mystery of lawlessness" is already working, the "Lawless One" (that is, Man of Lawlessness, Son of Ruin) will not be revealed so long as there is "holding fast."

What is "holding fast"? The King James Version translates the Greek word *kateko* as "withholds" or "restrains" in verse 6. The same word is translated in verse 7 in King James Version as "lets will let," or "hinders will continue to hinder." The Lie is operative here also, for the generally held interpretation of this passage is in error. For example, some scholars identify the restraining influence as the Holy Spirit. This view is supported primarily by presuming that *strives* of Genesis 6:3 means "restrains." Other opinions hold that the restraining influence is secular government, with specific reference to the Roman Empire. Still others interpret this to refer to persecution, which kept the church at Smyrna so as not to deserve rebuke; but, after the persecution disappeared, the church began to fall, a la Pergamum.

But we need not speculate as to the meaning. A specific Greek word (*kateko*) is used here. If we look at the subject and object of this verb in the nineteen places where it is used, and especially those usages in the epistles, I believe we shall see clear evidence of the meaning here. Moreover, another Greek word in 2 Thessalonians 2:7 is not properly translated; viz., "out of the way" should be "out of the midst." We shall look at this also.

Scripture Context	Subject	Object
1. Matt. 21:38—"This is the heir; come let us kill him, and let us *seize* [hold fast] his inheritance."	**Farmers in charge of vineyard who opposed their lord**	**Inheritance**

Scripture Context	Subject	Object
2. Luke 4:42—"And the people sought Him, and came unto Him, and would have *held* him *fast* [KJV—"stayed him"] that He should not depart from them."	People who sought Christ	Christ
3. Luke 8:15—"They who, in an honest and good heart, having heard the word, *hold* it *fast* [KJV—"keep it"], and bring forth fruit with patience."	Honest and good heart	Word
4. Luke 14:9—"Sit not down in the chief seat, lest... he that invited you come and say to you, 'Give this man place'; and you begin with shame to take [*hold fast*] the lowest place."	Wedding guest	Humble place

Scripture Context	Subject	Object
5. John 5:3–4—Impotent folk, blind, lame, paralyzed, who first stepped in was made well of whatever disease *held him* (KJV—"he had").	Disease	Impotent folk (blind, lame, paralyzed)
6. Acts 27:40—"They committed unto the sea . . . and *held fast* [KJV—"made toward"] to shore" (Acts 27:44—"they all escaped safely to the land")	Ship at sea	Shore/land (safety)
7. Rom. 1:18—"Wrath of God is revealed from heaven against all ungodliness and unrighteousness of men, who *hold fast* [i.e., "hold captive"] the truth in unrighteousness"	Ungodly men	Truth

Scripture Context	Subject	Object
8. Rom. 7:6—"Now we are delivered from the law, that being dead in which we were *held fast*, that we should serve in newness of Spirit"	Dead law	Unbelievers
9. 1 Cor. 7:29–30—The time is short . . . they that buy should be as though they do not *hold fast* (KJV—*possess*)	Those who would attend upon the Lord without distraction (1 Cor. 7:35)	*Not* things
10. 1 Cor. 11:2—"Now I praise you, brothers, that you . . . *hold fast* (KJV—*keep*) the teachings (NIV) as I delivered to you."	Brothers in Christ	Ordinances delivered by Paul
11. 1 Cor. 15:2 " . . . *hold fast* [KJV—*keep*] in memory what I have preached to you"	Brothers in Christ	Gospel (1 Cor. 15:1)

Scripture Context	Subject	Object
12. 2 Cor. 6:10—As "workers together with Him" (v. 1), as the "ministers of God" (v. 4), commend ourselves as "having nothing, and yet *holding fast* [KJV—*possessing*] all things."	Workers together Ministers of God	All things
13. 1 Thess. 5:21—"*Hold fast* that which is good"	Brothers in Christ (1 Thess. 5:12, 14)	That which is good
14. 2 Thess. 2:6—"And now you know what *holds fast* [KJV—*with-holds*] that he might be revealed in his time."		
15. 2 Thess. 2:7—"For the mystery of lawlessness does already work, only the [not 'he' as in KJV] *holding fast* just now until out of midst it comes."		

Scripture Context	Subject	Object
16. Philemon 13—"I beseech you for my son Onesimus [*profitable*] . . . whom I would have *held fast* [KJV—*retained*] with me."	Paul	Onesimus (*profitable*)
17. Heb. 3:6—"Christ as a son over His house, whose house are we, if we *hold fast* the confidence and the rejoicing of the hope firm unto the end."	Christ's House (Brothers in Christ; Heb. 3:12)	Confidence and hope unto the end
NOTE: This stipulation to hold fast the confidence and hope unto the end is immediately followed by "wherefore": ☐ "Today, if you will hear His voice, harden not your hearts" (Heb. 3:7–8; as the children of Israel, God's people, in the wilderness did). ☐ "They do err in heart and have not known my ways" (Heb. 3:10; I was grieved with that "generation"). ☐ "Take heed, brothers, lest there be in any of you an evil heart of *unbelief*, in departing from the living God" (Heb. 3:12).		
18. Heb. 3:14—"For we are made partakers of Christ, if we *hold fast* the beginning of our confidence steadfast unto the end."	Partakers of Christ	Beginning of our confidence

Scripture Context	Subject	Object
NOTE: This stipulation to hold fast the beginning of our confidence that we might continue as partakers of Christ is also immediately followed by: ☐ "Today, if you will hear His voice, harden not your hearts as in the provocation" (Heb. 3:15). ☐ "We see that they could not enter in [to His rest—Heb. 3:18] because of unbelief" (Heb. 3:19). ☐ "Let us fear lest we come short of the promise of entering into rest" (Heb. 4:1).		
19. Heb. 10:23—"Let us *hold fast* the profession of faith without waivering [for He is faithful that promised]."	Brothers in Christ (Heb. 10:19) House of God (Heb. 10:21)	Profession of faith
NOTE: "Holding fast" depends upon believing that God is faithful!		

Disregarding the four negative references (1, 5, 7, 8), we find there are fifteen affirmations that we are to *hold fast* to Christ, the Word, the humble place, the land (symbolic of safety, as distinguished from the sea of chaotic humanity), the gospel, the profitable, and, above all, to the *confidence* and *hope* (i.e., solid *expectation*) that God is faithful and keeps His promises. This is belief in the living God!

The *way* in 2 Thessalonians 2:7 is most everywhere translated "midst," meaning "in the middle of." For example, in Matthew we find:

10:16—"sheep in midst of wolves"

13:25—"tares among wheat"

14:24—"ship in midst of sea"

18:20—"there I AM in the midst of them"

The Messianic statement in Hebrews 2:12 uses this same word: "I will declare your name unto my brothers, in the *midst* of the church ['the called-out ones'] will I sing praise unto you."[6]

Most striking is the use of the term "midst" in Revelation:

1:3—"in the *midst* of seven lampstands"

2:1—"in the *midst* of seven churches"

2:7—"tree of life, which is in the *midst* of the paradise of God"

4:6—"in the *midst* of the throne"

5:6—"in the *midst* of the throne... stood a Lamb"

6:6—"in the *midst* of the four living creatures"

7:17—"Lamb who is in the *midst* of the throne"

22:2—"in the midst of the street of it... the Tree of Life"

The *midst* we are talking about is the "midst" from God's perspective. Note in Genesis 2:9 that God put the Tree of Life in the midst (the center) of the garden—the Tree of Knowledge of Good and Evil was in the garden, but, in God's sight, it was not in the center. Yet Eve, in talking to Satan, had developed such an attraction to, or fascination with, the Tree of the Knowledge of Good and Evil that she identifies it (Gen. 3:3) as being "in the midst of the garden." To face the Tree of the Knowledge of Good and Evil is to turn one's back on the Tree of Life; and then, for that person, the Tree of Life is no longer in the midst!

Hence, the meaning of 2 Thessalonians 2:6–7 becomes clear: The "mystery of lawlessness" (which corresponds to the "mystery of Babylon the Great" [Rev. 17:5] and the "mystery of the woman"

[Rev. 17:7], or self-love) is hindered so long as the church holds fast to its hope and keeps Christ in the midst, in the center.

All of the other "mysteries" (see Appendix C) identified in the New Testament are understood in the context of *agape,* or God's love. Self-love cannot effectively operate where Christ is in the center. When we leave from this "first love" (Rev. 2:4), then men become gradually more prominent and take the center position (that is, the deeds and doctrine of the Nicolaitans)[1] until the "mystery of lawlessness" (self-love) gains full sway.

Using as a guide several interlinear Greek translations, together with the understanding that we have obtained through study of the foregoing Scriptures, we see that 2 Thessalonians 2:6–7 should read as follows:

> And now the holding fast you fully know and understand, for him to be revealed in his time [in due measure or at the proper season]. For the mystery of lawlessness is already working [operating]; only there is the holding fast just now until out of the midst it comes [Greek—*ginomai*—signifying a changed condition or state].

Hence, so long as we hold fast to Christ, keeping Him in the center of the church, there is no falling away; but when Christ is taken out of the center, then the Lawless One is revealed (2 Thess. 2:8).

---

[1] *Nicolaitans* (Rev. 2:6, 15) is the Greek word *nicolait,* and is the combination of two other Greek words: *nikao,* meaning "conquer" or "above others," and *laos,* meaning "common people." So *nicolait* means "conquering the common people" or "climbing above the laity." *Nicolaitans,* then, refers to a group of people whose love of self causes them to esteem themselves higher than the common believers. At Ephesus it had already become a de facto practice (Rev. 2:6; *deeds*), but at Pergamum it had become enshrined as a doctrine (Rev. 2:16).

Presence (*Parousia*) of the Lawless One vs. Presence (*Parousia*) of the Lord

Lawless One's Presence	Lord's Presence
"And then shall that Lawless One be revealed... whose presence [Greek—*parousia*] is after the working of Satan with all power and signs and lying wonders" (2 Thess. 2:9).	"The Lord shall consume the Lawless One [in the Day of the Lord] with the Spirit of His mouth, and shall destroy with the brightness of His presence [Greek—*parousia*]" (2 Thess. 2:2, 8).

The key word here is *parousia*. Let's look at it.

Scripture Context	Situation	Result
1. Matt. 24:1–3—"Jesus went out, and departed from the temple... 'There shall not be here left one stone upon another, that shall be thrown down'... The disciples came to Him privately saying, 'When shall these things be? And what the sign of *your parousia* and of the end of the age?'"	Many shall be deceived by those who say, "I am Christ" (Matt. 24:5). Many false prophets shall deceive many (Matt 24:11). Love (*agape*) of many shall grow cold because lawlessness shall abound (Matt 24:12).	Bright shining over the whole world (Matt. 24:27). Gospel of Kingdom preached in whole world for a witness to all nations (Matt. 24:14).

Scripture Context	Situation	Result
2. Matt. 24:27—"As the *bright shining* (KJV—*lightning*) comes out of the east, and shines even unto the west, so shall also the *parousia of the Son of Man* be. For wherever the carcass is, there will the eagles be gathered together."	Great trouble (Matt. 24:21) False Christs and false prophets showing great signs and wonders (Matt. 24:24) The very elect shall be deceived (Matt. 24:24)	Bright shining over the whole world (Matt. 24:27)

NOTE: We must digress to consider "the carcass." The same statement appears in Luke 17:37 where it is translated: "Wherever the body is, there will the eagles be gathered together." The word *carcass* or "body" is the Greek word *ptoma,* which denotes, literally, "a fall"; hence, that which is fallen, a corpse (see Matt. 14:12, Mark 6:29, Rev. 11:8–9).

The statement in Luke 17:37 is an answer to the question, "Where will one be taken and the other left?" The "dead" will be the taken ones, for eagles feed on dead flesh (Job 39:27–30).

This discussion occurs in the context of an answer to the Pharisees' question, "When will the Kingdom of God come?" Jesus replied, "The Kingdom of God comes not with observation, neither shall they say, 'lo here!' or, 'lo there!' For, behold, the Kingdom of God is within you" (Matt. 24:23). This expression, "within you," occurs only one other place, in Matthew 23:26, "Cleanse first that which is *within* the cup and platter, that the outside of them may be clean also."

Let us keep this view of the Kingdom of God in mind as we consider, "What is the parousia?"

Scripture Context	Situation	Result
3. Matt. 24:37—"But of that day and hour knows no man, no, not the angels of heaven, but my Father only. But as the days of Noah [*rest*], so shall also the *parousia of the Son of Man* be."	"This generation [the 42nd generation] shall not pass till all these things be fulfilled" (Matt. 24:34). "Heaven and earth shall pass away, but my words shall not pass away" (Matt: 24:35). "Like the days of Noah" (Matt. 24:37).	Flood came and took all disobedient ones away (Matt. 24:39).

Scripture Context	Situation	Result
4. Matt. 24:38–39 —"For as in the days that were before the flood they were eating and drinking, marrying and giving in marriage until the day that Noah [*rest*] entered into the ark, and knew not until the flood came, and took them all away, so shall also the *parousia of the Son of Man* be."	Eating, drinking, marrying (Matt. 24:38) Sons of God married daughters of men (spiritual mixed with natural) and produced men of renown (great name) (Gen. 6:4).	Flood came and took all disobedient ones away (Matt. 24:39). Two shall be in the field: one taken and other left (Matt. 24:40).
ADMONITION: Watch that we may be found faithful (Matt. 24:42).		

Scripture Context	Situation	Result
5. 1 Cor. 15:23—"Christ is risen from the dead and become the first-fruits of them that slept" (v. 20). "For as in Adam all die, even so in Christ shall all be made alive" (v. 22). "But every man in his own order: *Christ the first fruits; afterward they that are Christ's at His parousia.*" "Then the end, when He shall have delivered up the Kingdom to God' (v. 24) "Be not deceived... awake to righteousness, and sin not; for some have not the knowledge of God. I speak to your shame" (vv. 33–34).	There will be *resurrection* of the dead (1 Cor. 15:12–23)	Resurrection shall occur at *parousia.* When death is destroyed, Kingdom shall be delivered to the Father (1 Cor. 15:24, 26)
ADMONITION: Be not deceived. Awake to righteousness and sin not.		

Scripture Context	Situation	Result
6. 1 Cor. 16:17—"I am glad of the *parousia* of Stephanas [*crowned*], and Fortunatus [*well freighted*], and Achaicus [*wailing*] . . . They have refreshed my spirit."	Paul had need (1 Cor. 16:17) House of Stephanas is devoted to ministry of the saints in love (1 Cor. 16:14–15)	Their personal presence refreshed Paul's spirit
NOTE: The letter to 1 Corinthians ends with this admonition: "If any man love not the Lord Jesus Christ, let him be anathema ('accursed'); maranatha ('our Lord comes')."		
7. 2 Cor. 7:6—"God, who comforts those that are cast down, comforted us by the *parousia* of Titus [*nurse* or *rearer*]."	Flesh had no rest (2 Cor. 7:5) Troubled on every side (2 Cor. 7:5) Fightings without, fears within (2 Cor. 7:5)	Comfort through the personal presence of Titus (compare to Isa. 49:13–15)

Scripture Context	Situation	Result
8. 2 Cor. 7:7—“Not by [*Titus*] *parousia* only, but by the consolation with which he was comforted in you,” when he told me of your loving/caring attitude toward me.	Paul had to rebuke Corinthians for sin (2 Cor. 7:8–10)	Repentance and rejoicing
9. 2 Cor. 10:10—Paul’s letters are weighty and powerful, but his bodily *parousia* is weak.	Paul does not commend himself (2 Cor. 10:12) He that glories, let him glory in the Lord (2 Cor. 10:17)	He that commends himself is not approved, but he that the Lord commends (2 Cor. 10:l8)

Scripture Context	Situation	Result
10. Phil. 1:26—"Having this confidence, I know that I shall abide and continue with you all for your furtherance and joy of faith, that your rejoicing may be more abundant in Jesus Christ for me by my *parousia* to you again."	To live is Christ; to die is gain (Phil. 1:21)	Rejoicing more abundant (Phil. 1:26)
ADMONITION: Stand fast in one spirit, with one mind striving together for the faith of the gospel (Phil. 1:27).		
11. Phil. 2:12—"As you have always obeyed, not as in my *parousia* only, but now much more in my absence, work out your own salvation with fear and trembling.	Obey (Phil. 2:12) Work out your salvation (Phil. 2:12) Do all things without murmuring (Phil. 2:14) Holding forth word of life (Phil. 2:16)	Shine as lights in the world in the midst of crooked and perverse generation (Phil. 2:15) I will rejoice (Phil. 2:16)

Scripture Context	Situation	Result
12. 1 Thess. 2:19—"What is our hope, or joy, or *crown of rejoicing*? Are not even you when we stand before (KJV—*in the presence of*) our Lord Jesus Christ at His *parousia*? For you are our glory and joy."	You received the Word in much affliction with joy of the Holy Spirit (1 Thess. 1:6; 2:14–16)	Hope Joy Crown of rejoicing
13. 1 Thess. 3:13—"To the end He may establish your hearts unblameable in holiness before God, even our Father, at the *parousia of our Lord Jesus Christ with all His saints.*"	Increase and abound in love (1 Thess. 3:12)	Blameless in holiness
NOTE: This is not just His personal presence (parousia), but His personal presence "*with all His saints.*"		

Scripture Context	Situation	Result
14. 1 Thess. 4:15—"For this we say unto you by the word of the Lord, that we who are alive and remain unto the *parousia of the Lord* shall not precede them who are asleep."	Sorrow for those who sleep (1 Thess. 4:13)	Dead in Christ shall rise first (1 Thess. 4:16) Rest shall be caught up together with them in clouds (1 Thess. 4:17) So shall we ever be with the Lord (1 Thess. 4:17)
NOTE: It is "in clouds," not "in the clouds." When compared to the preceding (1 Thess. 3:13), it is not unlikely that the "clouds" are the saints.		
15. 1 Thess. 5:23—"God of peace sanctify you wholly; and your whole spirit and soul and body be preserved blameless unto the *parousia of the Lord Jesus Christ.* Faithful is He who calls you, who will also do it."	God sanctify you wholly	Preserved blameless for God is faithful

Scripture Context	Situation	Result
16. 2 Thess. 2:1—"We beseech you brothers by the *parousia of our Lord Jesus Christ*... that you not soon be shaken in mind, or troubled... as that the Day of the Lord is present."	Thessalonians feared that they had missed the *parousia* and were now experiencing the Day of the Lord. (Compare to 2 Thess. 2:4; "persecutions and tribulations that you endure.")	Gathering together unto Him (2 Thess. 2:1)
ADMONITION: Warning not to be deceived, for there shall be a "falling away" *before parousia*.		
17. 2 Thess. 2:8—Lord shall destroy the Lawless One with brightness of *His parousia*.	Lawless One is uncovered/revealed	Lawless One will be destroyed

Scripture Context	Situation	Result
18. 2 Thess. 2:9—"The Lawless One shall be revealed whose *parousia* is after the working of Satan [i.e., according to the operation of Satan]."	No love of the truth (2 Thess. 2:10)	Deceivableness of unrighteousness (2 Thess. 2:10) Belief in The Lie (2 Thess. 2:11) All will be judged (KJV—*damned*) (2 Thess. 2:12)
19. James 5:7—"Be patient therefore, brothers, unto the *parousia of the Lord*."	Patience	Precious fruit
20. James 5:8—"Be you also patient [like the farmer], establish your heart; for the *parousia of the Lord* draws near."	Patience (James 5:8) Endurance (James 5:11)	Judge stands before the door (James 5:9)

Scripture Context	Situation	Result
21. 2 Peter 1:16—“We have not followed cunningly devised fables when we made known unto you the power [*dunamis*] and *parousia of our Lord Jesus Christ*, but *were eyewitnesses* of His majesty.”	Transfiguration (Matt. 17:1–5) Face did shine as the sun “This is my beloved Son in whom I am well pleased; hear Him”	Majesty Honor and glory
NOTE: Peter was an eyewitness of *parousia*.		
22. 2 Peter 3:3–4—“There shall come in the last days scoffers, walking after their own lusts, and saying, ‘Where is the *promise of his Parousia*?’ “Be not ignorant that one day is with the Lord as a thousand years” (2 Pet. 3:8).	Impatience (2 Pet. 3:4) Scoffers (2 Pet. 3:3) Lusts (2 Pet. 3:3)	Judgment by fire (2 Pet. 3:7) Ruin (2 Pet. 3:7)
ADMONITION: Be not ignorant concerning the timing of *parousia*.		

Scripture Context	Situation	Result
23. 2 Peter 3:12—"Looking for and hasting unto the *parousia of the day of God*, in which the heavens being on fire, shall be dissolved... Nevertheless we, according to His promise, look for new heavens and a new earth, in which dwells righteousness."	Day of the Lord will come as a thief in the night (2 Pet. 3:10)	Works shall be burned (2 Pet. 3:10) New heavens and new earth (2 Pet. 3:13)
ADMONITION: "Be diligent to be found in peace, without spot, and blameless" (2 Pet. 3:14).		
24. 1 John 2:28—"And now, little children, abide in Him, that, when He shall appear, we may have confidence and not be ashamed before Him at *His parousia*."[1]	Antichrist seduces (1 John 2:22, 26) Anointing abides in you (1 John 2:27)	Confidence OR Shame[1]
ADMONITION: Abide in Him (1 John 2:28). Purify yourself (1 John 3:3).		

[1] To be "ashamed" is to be naked and/or without suitable garments (Rev. 3:18).

Parousia means "personal presence." As we consider these passages, we note that only one refers to the Lawless one (the corporate Satan); six ("the number of man") refer to men like Paul, Titus, and Stephanas; seventeen refer to the Lord Jesus Christ, including three as the Son of Man (#2, 3, 4) and one (#21) with respect to His transfiguration.

It is not, I am sure, insignificant that there are seventeen usages of *parousia* with respect to the Lord Jesus Christ. Seventeen is not a multiple of any other number; it is seventh in the list of prime numbers. Seventeen connotes "the perfection of spiritual order," such as in Romans 8:35–39 where seventeen specific things are mentioned which cannot separate us from the love of Christ.

The number 17 is associated with "feeding the flock and being loved" (Genesis 37:2–4), with "windows of heaven opened in judgment" (Genesis 7:11), with the "rest and safety of God's people" (Genesis 8:4), and most significantly, with the fact that "nothing is too hard for God, so that we are assured that 'they shall be My people, and I will be their God'" (Jeremiah 32:9, with 32:14–15, 17, 27, 38).

Parousia of Christ

Parousia is somewhat of a problem. There is good reason to believe that Jesus is present with us now, for He is Immanuel, "God with us." Moreover, wherever two or three are gathered together in His name, He is in the midst (Matt. 18:20). We, as His body, are the fullness of Him who fills all in all (Eph. 1:23; Col. 2:10). Christ is in you, the hope of glory (Col. 1:27). He has promised never to leave us nor to forsake us (Heb. 13:5). Further, we have already demonstrated that the corporate Son of Man, of which Jesus is the Head, is here now! Also, the Son of Ruin, which is Satan's counterpart, is clearly present now.

Yet, at the same time, the references associating the Lord Jesus Christ and the Son of Man with parousia, except only for 2 Peter 1:16, are clearly future with respect to fulfillment or events.

Jesus was present with the disciples for 3 1/2 years. There is no doubt about that. His parousia (personal presence) was among them daily. Yet this was not *parousia* in the scriptural sense as relates to Jesus, with one exception. As we have noted, 2 Peter 1:16 was a special and unique personal presence, denoted as *parousia*. This event, then, gives us the basis for understanding the nature of the future presence even while acknowledging that there is a present presence of the Lord among us.

The transfiguration of Jesus is described in each of the three synoptic gospels: Matthew 17:1–8; Mark 9:2–8; and, Luke 9:27–36. In each instance the event of the transfiguration is preceded by Jesus' teaching:

> If any man will come after me, let him deny himself, and take up his cross daily, and follow Me…Whosoever will lose his life for my sake and the gospel's shall find [save] it.

Associated with this are three somewhat different statements immediately preceding the transfiguration event:

- Matt. 16:27—"For the Son of Man shall come in the glory of His Father with his messengers [KJV—*angels*] and then He shall reward every man according to his works."

- Mark 8:38—"Whosoever, therefore, shall be ashamed of me and of my words in this adulterous and sinful generation, of him also shall the Son of Man be ashamed, when He comes in the glory of His Father, with the holy messengers [KJV—*angels*]."

- Luke 9:26—"For whosoever shall be ashamed of me and of my words, of him shall the Son of Man be ashamed, when He shall come in His own glory, and Father's, and of the holy messengers [KJV—*angels*]."

Then, in each case, Jesus says, "There are some standing here, who shall not taste of death, till they see the Son of Man coming in His Kingdom." These "some" were Peter, James, and John who were witnesses to the transfiguration, which Peter describes as the *parousia*, which was a manifestation of power, majesty, honor, and glory (2 Peter 1:16–17).

Let us look at the details of the transfiguration, or *parousia*, of the Lord Jesus Christ as recorded in the three gospel accounts.

	Matthew	Mark	Luke
When	After six days	After six days	After eight days
Where	High mountain	High mountain	Mountain; to pray
Event	Face did shine like sun Raiment white as light Moses and Elijah talking with Him	Raiment became shining, exceeding white like snow as no fuller (Mal. 3:2) on earth can whiten them Elijah with Moses, talking with Jesus	Appearance of His countenance altered; His raiment white and glistening Moses and Elijah who appeared in glory and spoke of His departure

	Matthew	Mark	Luke
Disci-ples	Peter: "Let us make three booths"	Peter: "Let us make three booths" For he did not know what to say Very much afraid	Heavy with sleep When awake, saw His glory Peter: "Let us make three booths" Not knowing what he said Feared as they entered into the cloud
God	Voice out of bright cloud: "This is my beloved son in whom I am well pleased; hear you him."	"This is my beloved son; hear him"	"This is my beloved son; hear him"
Disci-ples	Fell on their face Very much afraid		
Jesus	Touched them and said, "Arise, be not afraid."		
Climax	Saw Jesus ONLY	Saw Jesus ONLY with themselves	Jesus was found ALONE

At the *parousia* commonly known as Jesus' transfiguration, the presence of Jesus, who had been with them daily, became a different presence. It is important to notice, I believe, that Jesus did not come from outside the scene, but took the select disciples with Him. His appearance, the nature of His presence, changed before their sleepy eyes (compare to Rev. 3:18). That which came from outside the scene was the cloud that overshadowed them, even as the Shekinah glory overshadowed the priests at the dedication of the tabernacle and again at the dedication of the temple. The *parousia* of the Lord Jesus Christ is the dedication of the temple wherein God will dwell! The presence of Jesus among them became a different presence, the *parousia*. Note that this change was a bright shining—His face shined like the sun and His clothing glistened as was prophesied in Malachi 3:1–4, where it says that such glistening will be pleasing unto Jehovah.

Notice also that the *parousia* occurred on a high mountain, symbolic of a very spiritual place, and that Jesus' face was altered "as He prayed" (Luke 9:29). (Elsewhere we have discussed that, only as the church enters into the ministry of intercession on behalf of the church, will the culmination of events associated with *parousia* occur.)

The timing is also specific. In two cases it is "after six days," which corresponds to the exposition on time (six thousand years from Adam) previously given. It is not totally clear why the Gospel which presents Jesus as the Perfect Man (i.e., Luke) specifies "after about eight days," but the meaning of "8" ("new beginning" or "new order" of things) is consistent with the fact that, in the parousia, man is transformed into a new order of man, wherein corruptibility becomes incorruptibility. There is some reason for believing that it was at this point where/when Jesus Himself became incorruptible.

This understanding of *parousia*, as distinguished from His continuing presence among us now, is substantiated in the expression associated with the use of *parousia* in Matthew

24:27—the parousia shall be like the "bright shining" (Greek—*astrape*; KJV—*lightning*) that comes out of the east; that is, the sun. Similarly, in 2 Thessalonians 2:8 we see the description "brightness [*epiphania*] of His parousia." In other words, the whole world will be conscious of only one being; namely, the Christ, the Son of Man ("saw Jesus only").

There are five other usages of *epiphania*:

1 Timothy 6:14—which associates *epiphania* with incorruptibility (KJV—*immortality*), which in turn is defined as "dwelling in the light" which no (corruptible) man can approach unto.

2 Timothy 1:10—where *epiphania* (KJV—*appearing*) is equated to incorruptibility (KJV—*immortality*).

2 Timothy 4:1—where *epiphania* (KJV—*appearing*) is associated with the Kingdom.

2 Timothy 4:8—where a "crown of righteousness" is promised to those who "love His epiphania." (KJV—*appearing*).

Titus 2:13—where *epiphania* is described as a "glorious" event wherein He will purify unto Himself a "people of His own" (KJV—*peculiar people*).

Even as we read these words, there is a revelation occurring that we may be the *parousia*; that is, our transfiguration, whether we have been awakened from the sleep of the grave, or shaken out of the drowsiness of Laodicea, will be the "brightness" of the *parousia*. At the *parousia* it appears that we shall experience (if we are found faithful) that which Jesus also experienced for He is described as "first fruits" in connection with *parousia* (1 Cor. 15:23).

Consideration of "the bright shining" (astrape) associated with *parousia* in Matthew 24:27 confirms this revelation. For example, in Luke 11:36, we see that a "whole body full of light" is as the "bright shining" (astrape) of a lamp. More significantly, in Matthew 13:41–43 we see these series of events:

> "All things that offend shall be gathered out of the Kingdom" (as tares are gathered from among the wheat and burned in the fire).
>
> Note: One more time we see that another aspect of "The Lie" is that the saints shall be gathered out; here it is explicit that the saints will remain, and the "things that offend" will be gathered out.
>
> "Things that offend . . . shall be cast into a furnace of fire."
>
> "Then shall the righteous shine forth [same *shine* as in "His face did shine like the sun" (Matt. 17:2)] as the sun in the Kingdom of their Father." (For with this Son of Man, the Father will also be pleased.)
>
> Note: See also Daniel 12:3; Malachi 3:18; 4:1–2; 1 John 3:2.

Readers, this is a good place to ask again if we deserve, as the disciples did, this commendation from our Lord: *"Blessed are your eyes, for they see; and your ears, for they hear!"* (Matt. 13:16).

The description in 2 Thessalonians 2:8 ("The Lord shall consume with the Spirit of His mouth and the brightness of His parousia") and the transfiguration as experienced, or witnessed, by the disciples also parallel another unique scriptural description—Revelation 1:12–18. Recall how the disciples, at Jesus' transfiguration, "fell on their face and were very much afraid." However, unlike those who shall be "naked" (Rev. 3:18) and "ashamed" (1 John 2:28), the disciples received a touch from Jesus and were told, "Arise, and be not afraid." Compare John's later experience:

> And I turned to see the voice that spoke with me...
>
> —REVELATION 1:12

> Out of His mouth went a two-edged sword; and His countenance as the sun shines in its strength.
>
> —REVELATION 1:16

> ...and when I saw him, I fell at His feet as dead. And He laid His right hand upon me, saying unto me, Fear not...
>
> —REVELATION 1:17

What is *parousia*? Parousia is the transformed presence of the corporate Son of Man, as distinguished from the corporate Son of Ruin. It is "our Lord Jesus Christ with all His saints" (1 Thess. 3:13). When this collective brightness shines, praise God, the Lawless One will be destroyed!

For some there shall not be the brightness of shining forth as the sun, and receiving commendation from the Lord; for these there shall be shame. Those born again persons who are not part of *parousia* will know, not glory, but *shame* (compare to Luke 14:9).

We are admonished to "abide in Him," and thereby to abide in love, that when He shall appear (phaneroo), we may have confidence and NOT be *ashamed* before Him at His *parousia* (1 John 2:28). *The shame shall be that, when He appears in the midst, we will be naked and not contribute to the brightness of parousia* (Rev. 3:18).

> Behold, I come as a thief. Blessed is he that watches, and keeps his garments, lest he walk naked, and they see his shame. And he gathered them together into a place called in the Hebrew tongue "Armageddon" [Hill of Slaughter]."
>
> —Revelation 16:15–16

The word *naked* is instructive. In Mark 14:51–52 we see one naked who fled from the presence of Jesus, whereas in John 21:7 Peter took care to clothe his nakedness as he ran toward Jesus. In 2 Corinthians 5:3–4 we read that nakedness is equated to mortality.

> Being clothed, we shall not be found naked. For we that are in this tabernacle do groan, being burdened; not that we would be unclothed, but clothed upon, that mortality might be swallowed up of life.

The word *shame* (*aschemosune*) which appears in Revelation 16:15 is used in only one other place. In Romans 1:27 it is translated "unseemly' with reference to homosexual relationships among men. The relationship between Christ (husband) and His church (bride) is clearly heterosexual. For example, in John 15:5 it is explicit that fruit is borne only of a union between Christ and His people: "He that abides in Me, and I in him, the same brings forth much fruit; for without me you can do nothing." When the members of the church enjoy just being with each other, rather than relating one on one to Jesus, it is a shame—and such shall be found wanting at parousia.

Parousia of Satan

The *parousia of Christ* will be His uniting on earth with His saints; that is, the Head will be joined to the Body, and there will be a collective brilliance, or shining, such that no man can withstand its presence.

The working of Satan seems always to precede the presence of Christ, both in type and in reality. For example, the lawlessness of Noah's day preceded the deliverance of the ark. The golden calf preceded the building of the tabernacle. The Babylonian captivity preceded the recovery of a remnant. And, the apostasy of the Pharisees, and Judaism generally, preceded the coming of Jesus.

We should not be surprised, therefore, to learn that the parousia of Satan in uniting with his sons will immediately precede the parousia of Christ. Yet, at the same time, the presence of the Lawless One has also always been with us. This mystery of lawlessness began to work (2 Thess. 2:7) from the moment that Christ was taken out of the center of the church, and was known from the time of John (1 John 2:18).

Bible numerics are helpful here also. The phrase "mystery of lawlessness operates" has a numerical value of "2040" (17 x 120).[7] The number "17"[1] indicates the perfection of spiritual order, and this is to occur in conjunction with "120," which means a "divinely appointed period of probation or test" (3 x 40). This may be somewhat puzzling, but, as we have intimated, it is the "mystery of lawlessness operates" that permits God's grace to be demonstrated in those who suffer as a result of the lawlessness.

For example, as we have seen, 2 Thessalonians opens with the exposition that "persecution and tribulation which you endure" (v. 4) are a manifestation, or sign, or token, that God considers us worthy of being tested, or proven, on behalf of the Kingdom of God (v. 5). And, in fact, He promises that those who inflict the tribulation will be recompensed (v. 6) when the Lord Jesus is revealed (i.e., at parousia; see v. 7). The fact that tribulation (trouble or suffering) will be the continuing lot of the saints is a frequent theme of Scripture (for example, 1 Peter 1 and Rev. 6:9–11).

---

[1] Recall that there are seventeen references to the parousia of Christ.

Continuing with Bible numerics, we find that the "Antichrist" of 1 John 4:3 ("which confesses not that Jesus Christ is come in the flesh"), which was already in the world, and "the great tribulation" of Revelation 7:14 both have the numeric value "2040."

1. What is tribulation? The word literally means "a pressing" or "pressure." It is anything that burdens the spirit of God's people. The first usage of the word *tribulation* (Greek—*thlipsis*) is found in Matthew 13:21 in Jesus' exposition of the parable of the sower's seed: "He that received the seed in stony places, the same is he who hears the Word, and immediately with joy receives it; yet he has not root in himself, but endures for awhile; for when tribulation [or pressure] or persecution arises because of the Word, immediately he is offended [that is, he is "trapped"—he can't stand the pressure]."

   The word *trapped* (KJV—*offended*) was, in the Greek, the name of that part of a trap, or snare, to which the bait is attached; hence, the word was sometimes used to refer to the trap or snare itself. "That day" (Luke 21:34–36) will come upon us as a snare unless we watch and pray always. In Revelation 2:14 Balaam's device to deceive Israel is the same word, *snare* (not "stumbling block" as in the KJV).

Let us look at the second and some subsequent usages of *tribulation*:

2. Matt. 24:9–11: "Then shall they deliver you up to be afflicted [to be pressured—to experience tribulation], and shall kill you; and you shall be hated of all nations [Greek word *goyim* means non-Israel peoples, or unbelievers] for my name's sake. And then shall many be offended [trapped, snared], and shall betray one another, and shall hate one another. And many false prophets shall rise, and shall deceive many. And because lawlessness shall

abound, the love [agape] of many shall grow cold."

It is interesting that some of those who deny the present working of the five-fold ministries (Eph. 4:11) assert that pastors are prophets!

3. Matt. 24:21: "Then shall there be great tribulation, such as was not from the beginning of the world to this time, no, nor ever shall be."

4. Matt. 24:29: "Immediately after the tribulation of those days… There shall appear the sign [*sign* is the same as "resurrection life" (Matt. 12:38–41)] of the Son of Man in heaven…and they shall see the Son of Man coming in the clouds of heaven with power and great glory."

Other references to tribulation include Mark 4:17; 13:19, 24; John 16:21 (KJV—*anguish*); 16:33; Acts 7:10–11 (KJV—*affliction*); 11:19 (KJV—*persecution*).

13. Acts 14:22: "…we must through much *tribulation* enter into the Kingdom of God."

14. Acts 20:33: "Bonds and tribulation [KJV—*afflictions*] await me [i.e., Paul]."

Additional references to tribulation include Romans 2:9; 5:3; 8:35; 12:12; 1 Cor. 7:28 (KJV—*trouble*); 2 Cor. 1:4, 8 (KJV—*trouble*); 2:4 (KJV—*affliction*); 4:17 (KJV—*affliction*); 6:4 (KJV—*affliction*); 7:4; 8:2 (KJV—*affliction*); 8:13 (KJV—*afflicted*); Eph. 3:13 (KJV—*afflictions*).

31. Phil. 1:16: "The one preach Christ of contention, not sincerely, supposing to add affliction [tribulation] to my bonds."

32. Phil. 4:14: "You have done well, that you did share with my affliction [tribulation]."

References also include Col. 1:24 (KJV—*affliction*); 1 Thess. 1:6 (KJV—*affliction*); 3:3 (KJV—*affliction*); 3:7 (KJV—*affliction*).

37. 2 Thess. 1:4: "Your patience and faith in all your persecutions and tribulations that you endure."

38. 2 Thess. 1:6: "It is a righteous thing for God to recompense tribulation to them that trouble you."

39. Heb. 10:33: "You were made a gazingstock both by reproaches and afflictions [tribulations]."

40. James 1:27: "To visit the fatherless and the widows in their affliction [tribulation]."

In Revelation 1:9, John identifies himself as our "companion in tribulation." In Revelation 2:9–10 tribulation is associated with "ten days," wherein "ten" is the number of "human responsibility." Those who remain faithful through the test of tribulation shall receive as a reward the "crown of life."

In both Numbers 11:19 and 1 Samuel 25:38 we see ten days associated with a testing, or proving, of God's people who have complained, or been foolish (*Nabal* means "foolish"). In Jeremiah 42:7, 10–12, we read:

> It came to pass after ten days that the word of the Lord came to Jeremiah: "If you will still abide in this land, then will I build you... Be not afraid of the king of Babylon, of whom you are afraid... For I am with you to save you, and to deliver you from his hand... And cause you to return to your own land."

Daniel himself suggests that the sons of God be tested for "ten days," and at the end of ten days their countenances were fairer than those who ate food provided by the King of Babylon (Daniel 1:12–15).

In Revelation 2:22 believers who commit fornication with the world will experience "great tribulation," but in the last and forty-fifth (5 x 9) reference to "tribulation," found at Revelation 7:14, we are told that those who come out of "the great tribulation" shall have "God dwell among them" (v. 15).

References to each of the forty-five scriptural usages of "tribulation" have been provided for information. If you will examine them all, you will note that in all but two instances (Rom. 2:9 and 2 Thess. 1:6) tribulation/affliction/anguish are associated with the people of God. This, of course, is contrary to popular opinion, but reflects yet another aspect of "The Lie." Our Lord Jesus would have us know that our hope is greater than tribulation (or trouble), and that this hope depends on His faithfulness. The Lawless One would have us believe, rather, that when the great tribulation begins, and rapture has not occurred, that we have been left behind. When hope is gone, we are his prey.

In Revelation 12:4 we see fair warning that his "tail" (*tail* means "false prophecy"; see Isa. 9:15) will draw away one-third of the saints ("stars of heaven"; see Genesis 15:5; Heb. 11:12 with 2 Peter 1:19). Hence, we are given the admonition in 2 Thessalonians 2:3: "Let no man deceive you by any means for [*parousia* (2:1) shall not occur] except there come the falling away first."

Notice the sequence of events in 2 Thessalonians 2:8ff. First there is the *parousia* of the Lawless One doing the works of Satan with "all power and signs and lying wonders." The result is an "operation of error" (KJV—*strong delusion*) causing "The Lie" to be believed. Then, shall be the "brightness" of the *parousia* of the Son of Man.

The "mystery of lawlessness" is pressure (tribulation) against those who are "lawful"; that is, against those who are submitted under the law of Christ, the law of love, making Him the center of their lives (1 Cor. 9:21—"without law" [lawless] vs. "under law"). This satanic pressure has always been with us. However, there shall be a "great pressure," or great tribulation, when

Satan is cast out of heaven (Rev. 12:4) for a special persecution of the church for 1260 days ($3^{1}/_{2}$ years). This will be Satan's *parousia*, when Satan will unite on earth with his sons, and constitute a great collective pressure, or tribulation, against the corporate Son of Man.

> These [the lawless one/the beast] shall make war with the Lamb, and the Lamb shall overcome them; for he is Lord of Lords, and King of kings, and they that are with him are called, and chosen, and faithful.
>
> —Revelation 17:14

Image of God vs. Image of Beast

Our Lord Jesus is the "image" (or manifest expression) of the invisible God (Col. 1:15; Heb. 1:3). No man has seen God at any time; the Son Jesus has manifested, or made visible, God before the eyes of men (John 1:18; John 14:9).

Christ, who is the image of God (lit. "the light of the gospel of the glory of God") gives us knowledge of the light of the glory of God in the face of Jesus Christ (2 Cor. 4:4–6), that we might, in turn, in Christ, be the image of God (Col. 3:10). However, "the God of this age" (KJV—*world*) has blinded the eyes of them who believe not (2 Cor. 4:4).

There is also an "image of the beast," made by man (Rev. 13:14–18), which is worshipped by man (Rev. 16:2). Whether we worship the beast (Rev. 19:20), or refuse to worship the beast (Rev. 20:4), determines whether we shall be cast alive into "a lake of fire" (Rev. 19:20) or "live and reign with Christ a thousand years" (Rev. 20:4).

The numeric value of "image of the beast" in Revelation 13:15 is "1840."[8] This is likewise the value of "Antichrist" in 1 John 2:22 wherein Antichrist denies that Jesus is the Christ; that is, "the Father and the Son." We are enjoined, therefore, to continue in the Son, which means to know that we are in Christ!

To continue in the Son is to continue in the Father, which is the promise of eternal life (1 John 2:21–25).

In effect, therefore, if we see Jesus Christ as anything other than the Son of God, we have created an image that distorts God's purpose for His people. It is instructive to note that the word *beast* is always used of "wild beasts," never of animals that could be used for sacrifices in the temple. For example, during Jesus tribulation, or testing, by Satan in the wilderness for forty days, He was "with the wild beasts" (Mark 1:13). In Titus 1:10–16 wild beasts (KJV—*evil beasts*) are equated with "unruly and vain talkers, specially they of the circumcision [i.e., Judaizers] . . . Who teach things which they ought not for filthy lucre's sake . . . They profess that they know God, but in works they deny, being abominable and disobedient, and unto every good work reprobate."

In 2 Thessalonians 2:9 the "working of Satan" refers to the activities associated with the beast: "power and signs and lying wonders."

Power (Greek—dunamis)

Consider also *authority* (Greek—*exousia*), frequently translated "power" by KJV.

> Rev. 13:2—"dragon gave him his power"
>
> Rev. 13:4—"dragon who gave authority unto the beast:
>
> Rev. 13:5—"authority was given unto him [beast] to continue 42 months"
>
> Rev. 13:7—"authority was given him [beast] over all kindreds, and tongues, and nations"
>
> Rev. 13:11–12—"another beast . . . who exercises all the authority of the first beast"

Rev. 13:15—"it was given unto him to give life unto the image of the beast"

Rev. 17:12—"authority as kings one hour with the beast"

Rev. 17:13—"power and authority unto the beast"

Rev. 18:3—"merchants of earth are grown rich through the power (KJV—*abundance*) of her insolent luxury or wantonness (KJV—*delicacies*)"

The first usage of *dunamis* is Matthew 6:13, "thine is the Kingdom and the *power*." Praise God, the last usage of *dunamis* is Revelation 19:1, where it is seen that all *power* is the Lord's who will have judged "the great harlot."

Signs (Greek—*seemion*) and lying (Greek—*psudos*) wonders (Greek—*teras*)

Where the words *signs* and *wonders* (*seemion* and *teras*) are used together in the gospels, they are associated with false prophets (Matt. 24:24 and Mark 13:22) and with unbelief (John 4:48). In all but two instances, in the New Testament *wonders* is always joined with *signs*. *Signs* occurs seventy-seven times, in only fifteen of which it is linked with *wonders*. *Signs* is clearly the dominant word and one to which we should give special attention.

The first usage of *sign* is in Matthew 12:38: "We would see a sign." This reminds us that people are always looking for the visible and external—something that satisfies the flesh. But Jesus responds in Matthew 12:39 by emphasizing that the only sign to be given is the sign of resurrection.

> There shall no sign be given to it ([the evil and adulterous generation], but the sign of the prophet Jonah.
>
> —MATTHEW 12:38–40; 16:1–4; LUKE 11:29–32

> For there shall arise false christs, and false prophets [that is, lying Christs and lying prophets], and shall show great signs and wonders, insomuch that, if possible, they shall deceive the very elect.
>
> —Matthew 24:24; Mark 13:22

In KJV the phrase "if it were possible" contains the "it were" in italics for these do not appear in the Greek text. They will deceive us if they can, if we let them!

Now note particularly that in Matthew 24:30, "immediately after the tribulation of those days," then shall appear:

> The sign of the Son of man in heaven.

What is this sign? Jesus gives us a specific definition. It is the sign of resurrection, which is *parousia*. Glory to God!

Since there seems to be a law of opposites as we compare the Son of Man and the Lawless One, the signs and wonders of Antichrist shall be opposite—not resurrection either actually or typically, but bondage under the law, with death as the result. Not a sign in the heavenly realm, but the Lawless One shall point to signs on earth.

The working of the Lawless One, who is the Beast, is with all "deceivableness of unrighteousness in them that perish [are ruined], because they received not the love [agape] of the truth, that they might be saved [rescued/delivered]" (2 Thess. 2:10).

There really is no excuse for the person who believes The Lie. We believe The Lie when we don't love The Truth! But why, or how, could someone who has been born again allow himself to be deceived? In other words, what causes us to fall from "first love"?

In the expression "deceivableness of unrighteousness" we see the pattern. This phrase literally translated means "deceit of unrighteousness," or "unrighteousness' deceit." The source of deceit is unrighteousness. Hence, in 2 Thessalonians 2:12 we see that the reason the truth is not believed is because there is "pleasure in unrighteousness."

There is an interesting contrast in the use of the word *unrighteousness* as relates to Jesus in John 7:16–18 and as relates to Judas Iscariot in Acts 1:18. Jesus, the Son of Man, teaches:

Righteousness	Unrighteousness
"My doctrine is not mine, but His that sent me"	**"Speaks of himself"**
"Seeks His glory that sent him"	**"Seeks his own glory"**

In Acts 1:17–18 we read that Judas Iscariot, the Ruined Son, "purchased a field with the reward of unrighteousness" (KJV—*reward of iniquity*). Judas was numbered with the company of Christ, but he sought his own glory.

Other definitions of "unrighteousness" include:

- Acts 8:23—trying to purchase the gift of God with money
- Romans 2:8 —"contentious and do not obey the truth"
- Romans 6:3—not yielding oneself to God
- 1 Corinthians 13:6—opposite of truth
- 2 Timothy 2:19—unrighteousness (KJV—*iniquity*) is "youthful lusts" (v. 22); "foolish and unlearned questions that breed strifes" (v. 23); striving (v. 24)
- James 3:6—"tongue is a fire, a world of unrighteousness [KJV—*iniquity*]," equating to "bitter envying and strife in your hearts," which is source of confusion (vv. 14, 16); whereas "fruit of righteousness" is wisdom from above

> that is pure, peaceable, gentle, easy to be entreated, full of mercy and good fruits, without partiality and without hypocrisy (v. 17)

In brief, unrighteousness is the opposite of all that God is, which is love as manifested in the fruits of the Spirit: love, joy, peace, longsuffering, gentleness, goodness, faith, meekness, and self-control (Gal. 5:22–23).

The word *deceivableness*, or *deceit*, means to "cheat, deceive, beguile"; in other words, that which gives a false impression, whether by appearance, statement, or influence. "Deceivableness of unrighteousness" is, therefore, opposite the nature, and contrary to the will of God, but which gives the appearance of being like God, of being for God. Deceit is subtle, and *the worst kind of deceit is self-deceit.*

The word *deceivableness*, or *deceit*, is used only seven times in the New Testament. A study of these seven passages shows the progression involved in falling away from truth into the "deceit of unrighteousness" unto believing The Lie. Let us consider these usages in terms of the subject doing the deceiving, the *object*, or truth, that is being undermined, and what is the result in the life of the believer.

Scripture	Subject	Action	Object	Result
1. Matt. 13:22	Riches	Choke	The Word	Unfruitful
2. Mark 4:19	Riches	Choke	The Word	Unfruitful
3. Eph. 4:22	Lusts	Corrupt	Manner of life	Unclean-ness with greediness

Scripture	Subject	Action	Object	Result
4. Col. 2:8	Philosophy Tradition of men Rudiments of world	Spoil (lit. "to carry off as a captive")	You	"Not after Christ"
5. 2 Thess. 2:10	Lawless One	Power Signs Lying wonders	Those who don't love the truth	Perish (that is, ruined, or loss of well-being)
6. Heb. 3:13	Sin (lit. "missing of the mark")	Hardening	You	Not entering into His rest (vv. 17–19)
7. 2 Pet. 2:13	Walk after flesh Despise government	Speak evil of things that they don't understand	Ourselves!	Perish (be ruined) in their own corruption Receive the reward of unrighteousness

Scripture	Subject	Action	Object	Result
7. 2 Pet. 2:13	Presumptuous Self-willed Speak evil of dignities (*dignities* refers to that which truly deserves worship)	Reveling with their own deceivings while they feast with believers Exercise with covetous practices	Others whom they promise liberty, but instead bring into bondage (v. 19)	Better for them not to have known the way of righteousness Dog is turned again to his own vomit (v. 22)

It is especially significant that the deception begins with "choking the Word." This confirms, in effect, the great tragedy that a person can be deceived even as he is being born again, if he is being fed a choked Word. (Compare to: "While they promise them liberty... [they bring them] in bondage" [2 Pet. 2:19]). Also, "Who has bewitched you?... Having begun in the Spirit, are you now made perfect by the flesh?" (Gal. 3:1–3).

Note that the choking of the Word is cited twice in only seven references. Note that it is the concern of the church with money that causes the choking. And, note that the result of the choking is nothing dastardly, at least not in terms of the human perspective. Those who are choked simply become "unfruitful"—that is, lives do not produce and manifest the fruits of the Spirit.

As noted previously, the absence of fruit results when the church acts homosexual. That is, man glorifies man. For example, folks are attracted to church meetings for reasons other than encountering the living Christ. A pretty picture of the preacher, or the opportunity to play on a softball team, is perceived as more of a motivation to attend than the presence of Christ "in the midst."

One of the vivid personal experiences I have had, which I can visualize today as clearly as the day it occurred many years ago, related to my dismissal from a local pastorate by a district superintendent of one of the evangelical denominations. Involved was a requirement for me to make a pledge I could not make, because I considered that it was contrary to Scripture.

During the course of three separate meetings over the course of several months in three different cities, not once was I asked to cite the Scriptures which were the basis of my opinion; nor were Scriptures cited to me as an explanation of the denomination's policy. Rather, I was told by the district superintendent that, although I was doing an excellent job (for attendance and giving had greatly increased during my pastorate), he would lose his position if he kept me—for the headquarters had spoken!

When the Word is choked, then human desires assure that our manner of life is not pleasing to the Lord. In lieu of the Word, philosophy, tradition of men, and the rudiments (that is, the elementary principles from which other things are derived) of the world implant us in a body which is not the body of Christ.

The ultimate deception is self-deception wherein each man becomes his own sovereign "reveling with their own deceivings while they feast with you" (that is, as they participate fully as part of the church; see 2 Peter 2:13–22).

This is the "image of the Beast," or the "image of the Lawless One," where each man lives according to his own opinion—hence, Laodicea, which means the "sayings or opinions of the people."

> For it had been better for them not to have known the way of righteousness than, after they have known, to

> turn from the holy commandment [love God; love one another][1] delivered unto them."
>
> —2 PETER 2:21

> But it happened unto them according to the true proverb "the dog is turned to his own vomit again; and the sow that was washed [John 13:10], to her wallowing in the mire.
>
> —2 PETER 2:22

> So, then, because you are lukewarm, and neither hot nor cold, I will spew you out of my mouth.
>
> —REVELATION 3:16

Operation of Error vs. Love of the Truth

The seven scriptures associated with "deceit" show clearly that the result of deception can be total ruin. The very repetitiveness of this theme, not only in 2 Thessalonians, chapter 2, but also throughout the Scriptures, should be sufficient warning to each who thinks he stands, to take heed lest he fall.

Love of truth is love of God! It is that simple. Second Corinthians 11:3 expresses Paul's fear, "Lest by any means, as the serpent beguiled Eve through his craftiness [KJV—*subtlety*], so your minds should be corrupted from the *simplicity that is in Christ.* For if he that comes preaches *another Jesus*... You might well bear with him [that is, support, encourage, forbear, or otherwise abet]..."

Paul is concerned because The Lie can be made very attractive and appealing. In fact, he says that false apostles and deceitful workers "transform themselves into apostles of Christ. And no marvel [that is, you shouldn't be surprised at this!]; for Satan

---

[1] Jesus' holy commandment was two injunctions: "Love the Lord your God with all your heart" and "Love your neighbor as yourself" (Mark 12: 30–31)

himself is transformed into an angel of light. Therefore, it is no great thing if his ministers also be transformed as the ministers of righteousness, whose end shall be according to their works" (2 Cor. 11:13–15).

In Ephesians 6:5 and Colossians 3:22 servants are enjoined to be obedient to their masters "in singleness of heart [*simplicity of heart*, same word as 2 Cor. 11:3] *as unto Christ... doing the will of God from the heart.*"

When the heart is in control, the mind (the knowledge of good and evil) is made inoperative. Now, this thought is anathema to human nature. But the fact remains that single-hearted loyalty, whether of child to parent, wife to husband, ball player to coach, soldier to general, or Christian to Christ, can only be present where the thinking process (the mind) is absent. When the mind begins to function independently, albeit, initially, sympathetically, the mind becomes open to the "working of error." When this happens, as is recorded in Romans with respect to the initial fall, God gives up man to his own "reprobate mind" (Rom. 1:28).

The same principle has been applied by God with respect to the second fall, wherein those who have become new creatures in Christ (the second Adam) have departed from their first love ("God is love" = "God is truth"; see 1 John 4:8; 1:5; John 3:33; 2 Cor. 1:18). "Because they received not the love of the truth... for this cause God shall send them "operation of error" (KJV—*strong delusion*).

What is *error*? The first use of the word *error* (Greek—*plance*) is very instructive. In Matthew 27:64 it is recorded that the Pharisees were concerned that the disciples might steal Jesus' body and claim that He was risen from the dead—"so the last error shall be worse than the first." Similarly, this very day the Lawless One robs God's people of their hope and expectation of glory by sealing the stone (the Word) and setting a watch. The watchmen not only do not necessarily point people to Jesus (Song of Solomon 3:3–4), but they try to wound us (Song of

Solomon 5:7) that we might stop seeking! Oh, that the people who are known by His name would read and study the Word for themselves—then there would be no error. If we stand fast in our liberty, then the "watch" can be made ineffective.

In the 1970s it was popular for Christians to assert that they were a "King's Kid." Many are even aware that we, ourselves, are indeed Kings in Christ (Rev. 1:6; 5:10; 1 Peter 2:9). But we live beneath our privileges unless we diligently search the Word of God.

> It is the glory of God to conceal a matter, but the honor of kings to search out a matter.
>
> —Proverbs 25:2

> He is a rewarder of them who diligently seek Him.
>
> —Hebrews 11:6

There is an example of a King exercising this prerogative in Esther 6:1. The King couldn't sleep. (God admonishes us to stay awake spiritually; see Ephesians 5:14.) In his sleeplessness the king began to search the "Book of Records." A direct result of the king's sleeplessness and his searching the records was survival of the chosen nation (Esther 6:11; 8:15–17); hence:

- Fulfillment of prophecy
- The coming of the Redeemer
- The whole work of redemption

Ephesians 4:13–14 makes it very clear that God's whole purpose is for His people to come "in the unity of the faith, and of the knowledge of the Son of God, unto a perfect man, unto the measure of the stature of the fullness of Christ." Christians should not be willing to settle for "unity of the Spirit," but should insist on seeking the truth so that there may be "unity of the faith."

The confusion of error has discouraged the body of Believers into accepting that The Truth will not be known until He comes—but what if He doesn't come until The Truth is known?

The confusion of error has caused man to believe that he cannot be perfect. Yet here in Ephesians 4, as elsewhere, it is stated as the explicit purpose of God that we might constitute one corporate perfect man unto the fullness of Christ (compare to Haggai 2:6–9):

> And He gave some apostles; and some, prophets; and some, evangelists; and some, pastors and teachers; for the *perfecting of the saints* for the edifying of the body of Christ, till we all come in the unity of the faith, and of the knowledge of the Son of God, unto a perfect man, unto the measure of the stature of the fullness of Christ... [That we] may grow up into Him in all things, who is the Head, Christ...
>
> —Ephesians 4:11–13, 15, emphasis added

Further, the Lord is explicit that we "be no more children, tossed to and fro, and carried about with every wind of doctrine, by the *sleight of men,* and *cunning craftiness,* by which they lie in wait to deceive" (lit. "in *inventing errors to mislead*").

The tragedy is that individuals who find Christ on the promise of deliverance from bondage are deceived, and led into greater bondage within the church. This is the meaning of 2 Peter 2:18, where Peter grieves that those "who are just escaping [KJV—*were clean escaped*] from them who live in error" are brought again into bondage (v. 19), and are again entangled in the pollutions of the world (v. 20). (Also see Galatians 5:1: "Stand fast in the liberty wherewith Christ has made us free and be not entangled again with the yoke of bondage.)

> For it had been better for them not to have known the way of righteousness than, after they have known, to turn from the holy commandment [Matt. 22:37-40; John 13:34] delivered unto them."
>
> —2 Peter 2:21

> Every spirit that confesses not that Jesus Christ is come in the flesh is not of God... By this we know the spirit of truth and the spirit of error... *he that loves not, knows not God; for God is love.*
>
> —1 John 4:1–10, emphasis added

Pleasure

What is *Pleasure?* In 2 Thessalonians 2:8 we read, "All might be judged (KJV: damned) who believed not the truth, but had *pleasure* in unrighteousness" is that which is pleasing or enjoyable. There are three kinds of pleasure referred to in the Scriptures.

1. Certainly the most significant is God's pleasure in His People (Ps. 147:11; 149:4; Rev. 4:11).

2. There is the pleasure of God's people wherein they delight in that which delights Him:

> Thou shalt arise and have mercy upon Zion; for the time to favor Her... is come. For your servants take pleasure in Her stones, and favor the dust thereof.
>
> —Psalm 102:13–14

In other words, God's people receive pleasure from the rest of God's people, even the simplest and least significant ("the dust thereof").

> Delight yourself also in the Lord, and He shall give you the desires of your heart.
>
> —Psalm 37:4

3. Then, there is also the pleasure that is alien to God's heart:

> You are not a God who has pleasure in wickedness.
>
> —Psalm 5:4

> God has not pleasure in fools.
>
> —Ecclesiastes 5:4

> God delights not in the strength of the horse; he takes not pleasure in the legs of a man.
>
> —Psalm 146:10

In other words, God does not delight in a man who stands on his own sufficiency.

> Believers who are deceived "count it pleasure to revel in the daytime."
>
> —2 Peter 2:13

> Those who believe not the truth have "pleasure in unrighteousness."
>
> —2 Thessalonians 2:12

The word *pleasure* in the Greek implies a gracious purpose, a good object being in view, with the idea of a resolve, showing the willingness with which the resolve is made. Altogether, there are twenty-one usages of *pleasure* in the New Testament. Let us look at them.

Scripture	Who Is Pleased	Object of Pleasure	Occasion	Result
1. Matt. 3:17	God	Son	Baptism with Holy Spirit	Led into wilderness
2. Matt.: 12:18	God	Son My Servant My Beloved	(Prophecy of Isaiah)	Spirit upon Him Justice to Gentiles
3. Matt. 17:5	God	Son	Transfiguration	The cross
4. Mark 1:11	God	Son	Baptism with Holy Spirit	Driven into wilderness
5. Luke 3:22	God	Son	Baptism with Holy Spirit	Led into wilderness
6. Luke 12:32	God	Seekers of the Kingdom (little flock)	Jesus teaching against hypocrisy—"leaven of Pharisees"	Give you the Kingdom
7. Rom. 15:25–26	Macedonian Christians	Poor saints at Jerusalem	Need of the saints of Jerusalem	Paul's journey

Scripture	Who Is Pleased	Object of Pleasure	Occasion	Result
8. Rom. 15:27	Macedonian Christians	Spiritual things	Need of the saints at Jerusalem for carnal things	Fruit
9. 1 Cor. 1:21	God	Foolishness of preaching	Destroy wisdom of the wise	To save
10. 1 Cor. 10:5	(See negative listing below)			
11. 2 Cor. 5:8	Paul	Absent from body Present with Lord	Walk by Faith	Labor to be accepted at Judgment Seat of Christ
12. 2 Cor. 12:10	Paul	Infirmities Reproaches Necessities Persecutions Distresses	For Christ's sake	When I am weak then I am strong
13. Gal. 1:15	God	Reveal His Son in me	Might preach among Gentiles	Conferred not with flesh and blood (in Arabia for three years)

Scripture	Who Is Pleased	Object of Pleasure	Occasion	Result
14. Col 1:19	God	In Him should all fullness dwell	Christ as Head of the body	Reconcile all things
15. 1 Thess. 2:8	Paul	Thessalonian Christians	Labor and travail among them	Impart unto you: • Gospel of God • Our own souls
16. 1 Thess. 3:1	Paul	Left alone at Athens	Could no longer forbear	Sending Timothy to establish and comfort you
17–20 (see negative listing below)				
21. 2 Pet. 1:17	God	Son	Transfiguration	Honor and glory

The ninth reference ("9" = finality = judgment and/or fruitfulness) tells the whole tale. That which is pleasing, logical, and natural for man is totally opposite to what is pleasing for God and for His people. To be associated with the glory of God is to face the cross (#3)—but what a climax to this transfiguration event when seen through the eyes of the Lord—not a cross, not suffering, but glory and honor (#21 = 3 x 7).

Those who are pleasing to God are led of the Spirit and find themselves in the wilderness (see #1, 4, 5, 13 in above chart). Do we find our "pleasure" in the Son? In the poor saints? In the spiritual things? In the foolishness of preaching? In infirmities? In reproaches? In necessities? In persecutions? In distresses? Let us each pray that God be pleased to "reveal His Son in me." There are four scriptures that identify objects of God's displeasure (see chart on next page). The last of the negative references to *pleasure* indicates that God is displeased when His children "draw back"; that is, they begin to doubt God's faithfulness.

"Draw back," or "withdraw," is a metaphor from lowering a sail and, as a result, there is a slackening of course; hence, being remiss in holding fast to the truth. The Greek prefix *hupo* means "underneath," adding the connotation of stealth, or a secret slackening of course.

There are other usages of the same word meaning "draw back" or "slacken course." In Acts 20:20, 27 Paul exhorts the Ephesian elders concerning the falling away and reminds them:

> I kept back nothing profitable for you.
>
> I have not held back [KJV—*shunned*] from declaring unto you all the counsel of God.

In Galatians 2:12, Peter "withdrew" and separated himself fearing the Judaizers (those who were of the circumcision). This is a good example of how knowledge of good and evil has resulted in division in the body of Christ.

In Hebrews 10:39, there is the noun form of the same word: "We are not of those who draw back unto perdition [ruin]."

Scripture	Who Is Displeased	Object Of Displeasure	Occasion	Result
10. 1 Cor. 10:5	God	Many of His children	Their lusting after evil things (the things of the world they had left)	Overthrown in the wilderness
(NOTE: The tenth position connotes "human responsibility"—they failed the test!)				
18. Heb. 10:6	God	Burnt offerings and sacrifices for sin	When Son comes to do His will as free-will slave (see Ps.40:6 with Exod. 21:5–6 and Deut. 15:16–17)	Law taken away
19. Heb. 10:8	God	Sacrifice and offering Burnt offering Sacrifices for sin	When offered by the Law When One comes to do His will	Law taken away
20. Heb. 10:38	God	If any man draw back	Parousia not yet come	Perdition/ruin

Returning to our basic Scripture text in 2 Thessalonians 2:12, we see, then, that having pleasure in unrighteousness is not necessarily reading *Playboy* magazine, or stealing money, or any other of the gross sins listed in Galatians 5:19–21 and elsewhere. (Lest there be any misunderstanding, we hasten to add that these are unrighteousness, too.) The point is, however, that the pleasure in unrighteousness that displeases God is hypocrisy—which is "playing church." It is not our gathering and assembling ourselves together, it is not our sacrifices of praise, it is not our deeds of charity, nor is it even our teaching and preaching that pleases God. What pleases God is our delight to do His will! Then, Christ is in the midst, and we feed on life.

Stand Fast

Following 2 Thessalonians 2:1–12, Paul leaves the negative and goes on to encourage. He is praying for the Lord to "direct your hearts into the love of God, and into the patient waiting for Christ" (2 Thess. 3:5). But he also gives a specific charge:

> To stand fast...
>
> —2 Thessalonians 2:15

There are eight exhortations to "stand fast" in the New Testament. The most interesting of these is the second, at Romans 14:4, where we are reminded not to engage in doubtful disputations with weaker brethren. The weaker brother, after all, is the Lord's servant, not ours. He is accountable to God, not us. Specifically, "to his own master he stands fast (KJV—stands), or falls. Yea, he shall be held up, for God is able to make him to stand."

The primary concern of each Christian, again contrary to popular teaching and practice, is to make sure that our own heart (not our brother's or sister's heart) is right before the Lord. Let us "stand fast":

Mark 11:25	Stand fast = Forgive
1 Cor. 16:13	Stand fast in the faith Watch Be strong Do all with love
Gal. 5:1	Stand fast in liberty
Phil. 1:27	Stand fast in one spirit With one mind Striving together for the faith
Phil. 4:1	Stand fast in the Lord
1 Thess. 3:8	Stand fast in the Lord
2 Thess. 2:15	Stand fast! = Sanctification of the spirit = Belief of the truth

Conclusion

The message of 2 Thessalonians, chapter 2, is not unique. Elsewhere in Scripture, if we have eyes to see and ears to hear, we will find the same message. While I was writing these words, I had occasion to sit under a teaching from Habbakuk and I was impressed that there in microcosm, we see the dilemma of Christianity today.

Habbakuk means "ardently embraces," or "he that embraces." The Lord Jesus Christ is available to be embraced in love. Jesus is willing to be "in the midst" of the church, to be in the center of my life, and your life. I can embrace Him ardently. It is my choice. The more I see of Christ, the more I will be grieved by the condition of the church around me, and I will cry out with Habbakuk, "Why?" "How long?" (Hab. 1:1–4; compare to Rev. 6:10–11).

The Lord's answer is that there shall be tribulation (pressure against the saints), even great tribulation, great pressure (Hab. 1:5–17). So Habbakuk set himself upon the tower, which means he surrendered himself into the hands of the Lord (Ps. 61:3; Prov. 18:10). The tower is in the midst of the vineyard which produces stinkberries (Isa. 5:2), and in the midst of the flock, the stronghold of Zion (Mic. 4:8). Habbakuk is prepared to receive reproof, which is instruction in the way of life (Hab. 2:1, with Prov. 6:23).

The Lord responded to Habbakuk in a vision (Hab. 2:1–4) indicating that the vision was not yet to be fulfilled—it was still future. However, God assured Habbakuk that, at the end, it shall be accomplished. God emphasized that the vision is *not a "lie"* (compare 2 Thess. 2:1–3). Then, God describes to Habbakuk two kinds of people:

1. One man has a soul that is lifted up (in pride), but which is not upright within him. This is the one who exalts himself in 2 Thessalonians 2:4 and Revelation 3:17, and therefore believes The Lie.

2. Another man lives by the faithfulness of God, and he is just.

Next God describes for Habbakuk the terror of the tribulation wherein "people shall labor only for fire (KJV—*in the very fire*) and the nations shall weary themselves for nothing" (Hab. 2:13). There shall be "nakedness" and "shame" (Hab. 2:15–17).

But, during it all, the Lord Jehovah is in His holy Temple (Hab. 2:20)! The terror and the horror of that which God will permit the nations to do to one another are described in living color (Hab. 3:1–15).

Habbakuk trembled at the description. His prayer is that he might "rest in the *day of trouble*" (Hab. 3:16). And he knows that he shall rest or stand fast. He will be in the midst of the trouble, meaning:

Fig tree will not blossom, and will be without fruit.

Olive labor will fail.

Fields will yield no food.

Flock will be cut off from the fold.

No herd will be in the stalls.

> *Yet will I rejoice in the Lord, I will joy in the God of my salvation.* Jehovah the Lord is my strength, and He will make my feet like hinds' feet, and He will make me walk upon mine high places.
>
> —HABBAKUK 3:17–19, EMPHASIS ADDED

What God is saying to His people is not a lie. Yet people prefer to believe The Lie.

In closing, let us take one more look at how The Truth and The Lie relate.

The love of God is the Love of Truth.

When Christ is not in the midst, there is not the love of truth (2 Thess. 2:10).

When we do not have the love of truth, we fall into believing The Lie (2 Thess. 2:11).

Once we have begun believing The Lie, we fall into disbelieving The Truth (2 Thess. 2:12).

Disbelieving The Truth means there are no longer any constraints upon us, and we find ourselves loving The Lie (Rev. 22:15).

Loving The Lie is making a lie (Rev. 22:15).

Let Him That Thinks He Stands Take Heed Lest He Fall

May the Lord bless to each of our hearts the life that is in these words. The Lord is calling us to prayer to intercede on behalf of His people. The more we see, the clearer our responsibility to intercede on behalf of those with lesser light, that we might all be brought into that glorious unity of the faith which our Lord has promised His people.

This is the truth and no Lie—that men ought always to pray, and not to faint.

> And shall not God avenge his own elect, who cry day and night unto him, though He bear long with them? I tell you that he will avenge them speedily. Nevertheless, when the son of man comes, shall he find faith on earth?
>
> —Luke 18:1–8

> The Pharisee stood and prayed thus with himself, "God, I thank you that I am not as other men"... The other man, Standing afar off, would not lift up so much as his eyes unto heaven, but smote upon his breast, saying, "God be merciful to me a sinner"... This second man went down to his house justified rather than the first man, for everyone that exalts himself shall be abased; and he that humbles himself shall be exalted... Whosoever shall not receive the Kingdom of God as a little child shall in no way enter it.
>
> —Luke 18:11, 13–14, 17

If any man loves not the Lord Jesus Christ, let him be anathema. Maranatha—our Lord comes!

4—Question

AFTER READING THIS book, I hope you have asked the question, "What does it mean for me?" If you have never been born again, have never asked Jesus to forgive your sins, and come into your heart, then what it should mean for you is, "It's time!"

This is the promise: "If you confess with your mouth, 'Jesus is Lord,' and believe in your heart that God raised him from the dead, you will be saved" (Rom. 10:9, NIV). Right now, where you are, bow your head and pray something like the following:

> *Lord Jesus, I know something is missing in my life. I need You. I confess that I am a sinner. I believe that You rose from the dead. Come into my heart. Cleanse me of all unrighteousness. From this day forward make me a new creature. Please direct me by Your Holy Spirit. Show me how to live my life. Hallelujah! Amen!*

If you have been born again, there are some deeper questions that you need to ask and answer.

- Where is Jesus in your life? In your church? Is He in the midst? Or is He on the sidelines grieving?
- Are you feeding from the Tree of Life, or from the Tree of the Knowledge of Good and Evil?
- Does your life exhibit the fruits of the Spirit—love,

joy, peace, long-suffering, gentleness, goodness, faith, meekness, self-control? Or are you given to disputation, criticizing, and judging? Do you throw rocks? Remember that Jesus asserted, judge not, lest you be judged!

- Do you recognize that there is only *one* church—a church without walls or rules? Remember, the church of Jesus Christ is not an institution or corporation, it is an extended family comprising the body of Christ with Jesus as the Head.

Most of us need to ask for forgiveness. Ask Jesus to direct your thought and action for His glory.

Have you progressed in your growth as a Christian? Are you increasing in spiritual wisdom and stature, and in favor with both God and man? Are you maturing into Sonship?

Have you ignored or disputed the revelations that God has given His church since he anointed Peter as the "rock" on which He would build the church? Do you follow men and traditions? Or do you follow Jesus, asking the Holy Spirit to instruct and guide you in each aspect of your life? In the Book of Acts, the epistle to the Ephesians, and throughout the New Testament, the fullness of God's gifts to His children is described. When the Mother Church ignored or lost what God had given at Pentecost, He began painstakingly to restore all of His truth according to the tabernacle pattern in the heavenlies. But these truths soon became branded with names and marketed as merchandise. Men who should have been leading His children into Sonship have instead led them into bondage.

The Lord hasn't given me a solution that I can provide to restore and cleanse the church, but I can urge that each of us needs to recognize that each Christian is, in some sense, in two "churches"—the true church (the city of Jerusalem), and the false church of Antichrist (the city of Babylon). The more we accept this realization, the more we will be open to the leading of the Holy Spirit, allowing Him to show us how to displace Antichrist. The sad thing is that the Book of Revelation clearly indicates that Antichrist will not go away. He will insist on bullying his way "into the midst." But let us buckle on the armor that God has given us: "the shield of faith," "the helmet of salvation," and "the sword of the Spirit, which is the Word of God" (Eph. 6:16–17).

One final thought: do not forget where we started—the fact that God has given our age two modern spiritual parables. The place to start if you are truly committed to displacing Antichrist in your local church assembly and in your life is with the messages of the parables.

1. Distinguish babies (those born again) from sons. Commit to rearing each newborn Christian into the fullness of Sonship. Lead them on the walk through the tabernacle (the heavenly pattern) from the altar of salvation, to the cleansing laver of the Word, to receive empowerment by the light (baptism) of the Holy Spirit at the lampstand. Then teach and encourage them to function as integral parts of the body of Christ at the table of shewbread, ministering to one another to edify/build up each member. "How is it then, brethren? When you come together, every one of you has a psalm, has a doctrine, has a tongue, has a revelation, has an interpretation. Let all things be done unto edifying" (1 Cor. 14:26). Enlighten them with the vision of the golden altar that, when the Spirit leads, all of the saints will commit to interceding for the final birthing of the church into the fullness of parousia!

2. Accept the fact that the church, and Christian behavior, has become homosexual—that is, man loving man, man obeying man, man receiving glory and praise from man. Determine to make your spiritual life heterosexual. The love relationship should be between man (bride) and Jesus (groom). Obey Jesus as He directs by His Holy Spirit. In other words, "Wait upon the Lord, and then

> he will renew your strength, and you will rise up with wings as eagles!" Finally, and perhaps most difficult for many of us, take the humble place. Exalt and praise Jesus. Displace the glorification of man that occurs in virtually every church, Christian broadcast, or book. In our daily interpersonal relationships may we seek to "serve one another."

As I was in the process of doing a final edit on the contents of this book, a remarkable thing happened. It was Sunday morning, January 14, 2006. I was standing as a member of the congregation in a local church building. It had no steeple, but the pictures and names of the pastor and his wife were prominently displayed. So there is a sense in which I was in Babylon. But, as I stood with others singing about the mightiness of God, the Lord forcibly reminded me of something I had been told more than forty years earlier.

A contemporary apostle of our Lord Jesus Christ, Erskine Holt*, had shared with me and others the account of a school teacher in a southern state in the late 1940s. She taught art, and there was one class she dreaded. The students in that class were physically and/or mentally handicapped, and

---

*Erskine Holt was one of the fathers of Pan America Mission, and had a retreat center in Zephyrhills, Florida, known as Corvilla. He constantly traveled around the United States and Colombia ministering in house churches, Bible study gatherings, and wherever he was invited. At his funeral in 2003 his daughter shared how Erskine always loved spontaneity and how he always encouraged everyone to be a participator of what God was doing in a meeting. Therefore, his funeral was conducted in an open platform setting, which meant that anyone could stand up and share what was on his or her heart during the service. He believed and practiced 1 Corinthians 14:26, "How is it then brethren? When you come together, every one of you has a psalm, has a doctrine, has a tongue, has a revelation, has an interpretation. Let all things be done unto edifying."

tended to be unruly. As she came to the door of her classroom one morning, her students were already inside, noisy and rambunctious as usual, already throwing brushes at one another. She stopped at the door and prayed something like this: "Lord, what am I going to do? I can't take this anymore." The Lord spoke to her, "I love these children. If you will look closely at each of them, you will see Me."

She went into the room, stood in front of the first student, and looked him squarely in the face. He was a hulking lad, but mentally handicapped. She looked at him and said, "Lord, I don't see You in him." The Lord said, "Look again. He is big and strong, and so am I." She went to another child, a meek little girl. Again she prayed, "Lord, I don't see You in her." The Lord said, "Look again. She is gentle, and so am I." During most of the remainder of that class period she went from child to child, looked in the face of each, and asked the Lord to show Himself in each.

When she was finished, she walked to the window and stood there looking out. She was tired. Then, behind her, there was a collective gasp of "Ahhhh!" from the children. She quickly turned, but saw nothing except "peace." The children were sitting quietly and were silent. She never again had any trouble from students in that class. Later she learned that, when she had faced the window and her back was to the students, each child had simultaneously seen Jesus in the midst. They had been instantly born again, and each one grew and matured to become a Christian adult!

On January 14, 2006, as I stood among Christians praising the Lord, my tears were freely flowing. When I tuned back into what was being sung around me, it was a spiritual song about needing Jesus more everyday. So as we close this book, let us each "turn your eyes upon Jesus, look full in His wonderful face, and the things of earth will grow strangely dim in the light of His glory and grace."[1]

Did you know that John 15:5 can be sung? "I am the vine, ye are the branches. He that abideth in Me and I in him, the same bringeth forth much fruit, the same bringeth forth much fruit, for without Me ye can do nothing!"

Let us see ourselves as Jesus sees us. But, above all, let's keep our eyes on Him. Then, there will be no place for Antichrist in the midst. The "midst" will be full of Jesus and His love.

Appendix A

Summary Descriptions of the Heavenlies

Type	1st Heaven	2nd Heaven	3rd Heaven
Numeric	1. Beginnings	2. Witness/ Separation	3. Divine perfection
Nature of God	Father's love (John 3:16)	Son's gifts (Eph. 4:8)	Spirit's revelation (John 16:14–15)
Tabernacle	Outer court	Holy place	Holy of holies (sanctuary)
Naturalist	Clouds (visible/ accessible)	Stars (functioning in the Spirit)	God's abode (place of the throne)
Understanding God	Jesus ("Jah Saves")	Christ ("anointed one")	Lord ("Jah," meaning "I AM")
Baptisms	Water	Spirit	Fire
Fellowship	…in the gospel	…of the Spirit	…of His sufferings
Effect on	Spirit	Soul	Body
John 1	See Jesus coming	They followed Jesus	Thou shalt see

Type	1st Heaven	2nd Heaven	3rd Heaven
Matthew 7:7–8	Ask…be given you ("things") (easy grace)	Seek…ye shall find ("Him") (diligence)	Knock… be opened unto you ("presence revealed") (absolute grace)
Location Types	Judah	Jerusalem	Zion
People Types	Saul	David	Solomon
John's Gospel	Chapters 10–13	Chapters 14–16	Chapter 17
Paul's Experience			2 Corinthians 12:1–10 —Abundance of revelations —Infirmities, reproaches, persecutions, distresses —Strength made perfect in weakness

Appendix B

Son of God and Son of Man

SON OF GOD

Devil/Test	Marvel at Work or Wonder	Source of Life	Negative (Lack of Life if Believe Not)
Matt. 4:3, 6	Matt. 14:33 (calm storm)	John 5:25	John 3:18
Luke 4:3, 9	Matt. 27:54 (centurion/earthquake)	John 11:4	John 9:35
		John 11:27	
		John 20:31	
		1 John	
		Hebrews	
	Mark 15:39 (centurion/earthquake)	Gal. 2:20	
Demons	**Resurrection**	**Water Baptism**	**Judgment**
Matt. 8:29	Romans 1:4	Acts 8:37	Rev. 2:18
Mark 3:11			
Luke 4:41			
Luke 8:28			

High Priest/ Mockers	Knowledge of Son of God Associated With Becoming Perfect Man	Water Baptism	Judgment
		Acts 8:37	Rev. 2:18
Matt. 26:63	Eph. 4:13		
Matt. 27:40, 43			
Luke 22:70			
John 10:36			
John 19:7			
	Witnesses		
	—Beginning of Gospel (Mark 1:1)		
	—John the Baptist (John 1:34)		
	—Angel to Mary (Luke 1:35)		
	—Nathaniel (John 1:49)		
	—Paul (Acts 9:20; 2 Cor. 1:19)		

There are twenty-seven usages of "Son of God" in the gospels (3 x 3 x 3; 3 x 9): Matthew (8), Mark (3), Luke (6), John (10). There are nineteen usages elsewhere, for a total of forty-six: 19 is the eighth primary number; 46 is 2 x 23; 23 is the ninth primary number.

Note: Number preceding each scriptural reference refers to the sequence in which that "son of man" reference appears in the New Testament.

SON OF MAN

Earthly Ministry		Against Him	
1—Matt. 8:20	No place to lay head	6—Matt. 12:32	Whosoever speaks word against, it shall be forgiven
2—Matt. 9:6	Authority to forgive sins	14—Matt. 17:12	Suffer of them
4—Matt. 11:19	Came eating and drinking	15—Matt. 17:22	Betrayed . . . kill him
5—Matt. 12:8	Lord of Sabbath (rest)	18—Matt. 20:18	Betrayed . . . condemn to death
8—Matt. 13:37	He that sows good seed	28—Matt. 26:2	Betrayed to be crucified
16—Matt. 18:11	Save that which is lost	30—Matt. 26:24	Betrayed
19—Matt. 20:28	Came to minister and to give his life	31—Matt. 26:45	Betrayed into hands of sinners
33—Mark 2:10	Authority to forgive sins	35—Mark 8:31	Must suffer
34—Mark 2:28	Lord of Sabbath (rest)	38—Mark 9:12	Must suffer
41—Mark 10:45	To minister and give life	40—Mark 10:33	Condemn him
47—Luke 5:24	Authority to forgive sins		

Earthly Ministry		Against Him	
48—Luke 6:5	Lord of Sabbath (rest)	44—Mark 14:21	Betrayed
50—Luke 7:34	Came eating & drinking	45—Mark 14:41	Betrayed to sinners
54—Luke 9:56	Not to destroy, but save lives	51—Luke 9:22	Must suffer
55—Luke 9:58	Nowhere to lay his head	58—Luke 12:10	Whoever speaks word against, shall be forgiven
66—Luke 19:10	Seek and save lost	62—Luke 17:26	As in days of Noah
77—John 6:27	Gives food which endures unto everlasting life	69—Luke 22:22	Betrayed
		70—Luke 22:48	Betrayed with a kiss
		80—John 8:28	Lifted up (on cross)
		84—John 13:31	Judas gone out; now is Son of Man glorified
Who do men say I am?		**We are hated for His sake.**	
10—Matt. 16:13	Man has reason to know	49—Luke 6:22	Blessed are you when men hate you . . .
82—John 12:34	Son of Man must be lifted up		
83—John 12:34	Who is this Son of Man?		

Heaven open/angels up and down		Sign of Jonah (three days in earth)	
73—John 1:51	Ye shall see heaven open	7—Matt. 12:40	Three days and three nights in earth
74—John 3:13	No man has ascended up but he that came down	29—Matt. 26:24	Go as written
What is Son of Man?		39—Mark 9:31	Delivered and killed
86—Heb. 2:6	That thou visitest him	43—Mark 14:21	Go as written
Sealed by Father		51—Luke 9:22	Rejected, slain, raised
77—John 6:27	Him has the Father sealed	53—Luke 9:44	Delivered into hands of men
Eat and drink flesh and blood of		56—Luke 11:30	Sign as Jonah to his generation
78—John 6:53	For life	65—Luke 18:31	All written accomplished
What if ye see Him ascend?		69—Luke 22:22	Go
79—John 6:62	To where He was before	72—Luke 24:7	Crucified, third day rise
		75—John 3:14	Lifted up as serpent
		82—John 12:34	Must be lifted up

Hour is come to be glorified		Raised from dead	
81—John 12:23	Son of Man should be glorified	13—Matt. 17:9	Tell no one until raised
84—John 13:31	Father also in Him	37—Mark 9:9	Tell no one until raised

Coming		Judgment	
3—Matt. 10:23	Son of Man be come	9—Matt. 13:41	Gather *out of* his Kingdom all things that offend
12—Matt. 16:28	Coming in His Kingdom	11—Matt. 16:27	Reward every man according to his works
20—Matt. 24:27	Coming as lightning	36—Mark 8:38	Be ashamed of them when He comes in glory with Father
22—Matt. 24:30	Coming in clouds... with power and great glory	52—Luke 9:26	Be ashamed of them ...
23—Matt. 24:37	Coming...as days of Noah	57—Luke 12:8	Shall confess before angels
24—Matt. 24:39	Coming...as when flood took them all away		

Reference	Description	Reference	Description
25—Matt. 24:44	Come at hour when don't expect—be ready	63—Luke 17:30	As in days of Lot when Son of Man revealed
26—Matt. 25:13	Watch—know not day or hour	68—Luke 21:36	Watch . . . pray . . . to be accounted worthy to escape and stand before Son of Man
32—Matt. 26:64	Sitting on right hand of power and coming in clouds	76—John 5:27	Authority to execute judgment
42—Mark 13:36	In clouds with power and glory	88—Rev. 14:14	Having on his head golden crown and in his hand a sharp sickle . . . and the earth was reaped
59—Luke 12:40	Comes at hour when don't expect—be ready		
61—Luke 17:24	Comes as lightning		
64—Luke 18:8	Will He find faith on earth?		
67—Luke 21:27	Coming in cloud with power and great glory		
11—Matt. 16:27	Come in glory of Father		

Glorified		Desire to see, but won't see	
81—John 12:23 84—John 13:31	Hour is come to be glorified Now is Son of Man glorified and Father glorified in Him	60—Luke 17:22	Days will come when ye shall desire to see one of days of Son of Man and you shall not see it (Kingdom of God comes not by observation)
Kingdom			
12—Matt. 16:28	Coming in His Kingdom		
		Right of God (stand)	
17—Matt. 19:28	Shall sit on throne of His glory	85—Acts 7:56	Standing on right hand of God

27—Matt. 25:31	Shall come in His glory and all his angels with Him, then sit on throne of His glory	73—John 1:51	Heavens open
32—Matt. 26:64	Sitting on right hand/ power	74—John 3:13	Who *is in* heaven
46—Mark 14:62	Sitting on right hand/ power	87—Rev. 1:13	Standing in midst of seven lampstands
71—Luke 22:69	Sit on right hand of power		
Sign in heaven			
21—Matt. 24:30	Then shall appear sign of Son of Man in heaven		

Usages of “Son of Man” in the gospels (84): Matthew (32), Mark (14), Luke (26), John (12); (2 x 42)(7 x 12)(6 x 14)(3 x 28). Additional usages in the New Testament (4, for a total of 88): Acts (1), Hebrews (1), Revelation (2); (2 x 44)(4 x 22)(8 x 11).

Appendix C

— Love—Key to the Mysteries

IN EPHESIANS 3:16–17, at the climax of the revelation of the truth concerning the ONE church, Paul prays a special prayer:

> That we might be strengthened with might by his spirit in the inner man that Christ may dwell in our hearts by faith.

There is an abiding there. There is a presence with a purpose, and the purpose is this:

> That you, being rooted and grounded in love, may be able to comprehend [grasp or understand]...

I set before you a proposition that understanding (or comprehending) of spiritual things depends directly and explicitly on a rooting and grounding in love (agape = godly love = charity). What we are to comprehend, in v. 19, is the "love of Christ." In other words, love comprehends love. Since God is love (1 John 4:8), it takes love to comprehend God. Since God is the Word (John 1:1), love is required to comprehend the Word. Hence, love is the KEY to the Mysteries.

- Mystery of Kingdom (Mark 4:11)
- Mystery of olive tree (Romans 11:25, in context of 11:13–25)
- Mystery of wisdom of God (1 Corinthians 2:7)

- Mystery of incorruption (1 Corinthians 15:47–57)
- Mystery of His will (Ephesians 1:9)
- Mystery of Christ (Ephesians 3:3–4)
- Fellowship of the Mystery (Ephesians 3:9)
- Mystery of Christ and the church (Ephesians 5:32)
- Mystery of the Gospel (Ephesians 6:19)
- Mystery of Christ in you (Colossians 1:26–27)
- Mystery of Christ (Colossians 4:3)
- Mystery of God, and of the Father and of Christ (Colossians 2:2)
- Mystery of Faith (1 Timothy 3:9)
- Mystery of Godliness (1 Timothy 3:16)
- Mystery of the seven stars (Revelation 1:20)
- Mystery of God (Revelation 10:7)
- *Mystery of iniquity/lawlessness (2 Thessalonians 2:7)
- *Mystery of Babylon the Great (Revelation 17:5)
- *Mystery of the woman (Revelation 17:7)

*While the key to each mystery is "love," it should be clarified that the key to these items (*) is self-love.

— Notes

Introduction

1. E. W. Bullinger, *Number in Scripture* (Grand Rapids, MI: Kregel Publications, 1967

2. Jerry Lucas and Del Washburn, *Theomatics* (New York: Stein and Day, 1977). Del Washburn has provided additional insight to the mathematical structure of the Scriptures in a later book, *Theomatics II* (Lanham, MD: Scarborough House, 1994).

3. Ibid., 19, 21.

Chapter 1

Modern Spiritual Parables

1. Clarence L. Barnhart, editor, *The American College Dictionary* (New York: Random House, 1953), 4.

2. Merlin R. Carothers, *Prison to Praise* (Escondido, CA: Merlin R. Carothers Publishing, 2005).

Chapter 2

In the Heavenlies

1. *The Englishman's Hebrew and Chaldee Concordance of the Old Testament,* fifth edition (Grand Rapids, MI: Zondervan, 1976), s.v. "heaven."

2. *The Englishman's Greek Concordance of the New Testament,* ninth edition (Grand Rapids, MI: Zondervan, 1976), s.v. "heaven."

Chapter 3

The Lie

1. Watchman Nee, *The Orthodoxy of the Church* (Anaheim, CA: Living Stream Ministry, n.d.).

2. Reprinted from *The Waning Authority in the Churches* by A. W. Tozer, copyright © 1995 by Christian Publications. Used by permission of Christian Publications, Inc., 800.233.4443, www.christianpublications.com.

3. *The Englishman's Greek Concordance of the New Testament,* ninth edition (Grand Rapids, MI: Zondervan, 1976), s.v. "apostasion."

4. Jerry Lucas and Del Washburn, *Theomatics,* 182. Additional information and more in-depth discussion is available in a later book by Del Washburn, Theomatics II (Lanham, MD: Scarborough House, 1994). The Institute for Theomatics Research has a Web site at www.theomatics.com.

5. Ibid., 77–79, 81, 83, 85, 88.

6. *The Englishman's Greek Concordance of the New Testament*

7. Jerry Lucas and Del Washburn, *Theomatics,* 183.

8. Jerry Lucas and Del Washburn, *Theomatics,* 184.

Chapter 4

Question

1. Helen H. Lemmel, "Turn Your Eyes Upon Jesus," public domain.